D0408795

Slackonomics

Slackonomics

GENERATION X

in the Age of Creative Destruction

By Lisa Chamberlain

Da Capo Press
A Member of the Perseus Books Group

 Printed in the United States of America. For information, address Da Capo Press, 11 Cambridge Center, Cambridge, MA 02142.

Designed by Brent Wilcox
Set in 11.25 point Apollo MT by The Perseus Books Group

Library of Congress Cataloging-in-Publication Data
Chamberlain, Lisa.
Slackonomics : generation X in the age of creative destruction / by Lisa Chamberlain.
p. cm.
Includes index.
ISBN 978-0-7867-1884-9 (alk. paper)
1. Generation X—Attitudes. 2. Generation X—Psychology. I. Title.
HQ799.5.C43 2008
305.2—dc22
2008006496

Published by Da Capo Press
A Member of the Perseus Books Group
www.dacapopress.com

Da Capo Press books are available at special discounts for bulk purchases in the U.S. by corporations, institutions, and other organizations. For more information, please contact the Special Markets Department at the Perseus Books Group, 2300 Chestnut Street, Suite 200, Philadelphia, PA 19103, or call (800) 810-4145, ext. 5000, or e-mail special.markets@perseusbooks.com.

10 9 8 7 6 5 4 3 2 1

For my mother,
who taught me very little about money
but a lot about creativity.

"Laugh now, but one day we'll be in charge."

—BANKSY, GRAFFITI ARTIST

CONTENTS

ACKNOWLEDGMENTS

First a huge thanks to Chris Carmody for your amazing support and advice throughout this entire $&(#*%! process. Whenever I was on the verge of a nervous breakdown or having a Jack-Nicholson-in-*The-Shining* moment with a bottle of vodka and an axe, you never failed to greet my call with: "Give me the pain."

I am also grateful to any number of other people and places, including Annie Price, whose friendship and support have been invaluable (I especially appreciate the apartment-sitting gig in West Hollywood and for loaning me some scratch at a crucial moment—I'll be paying that back any minute!). Amy Simpson, you are the best; I finally forgave you for leaving New York when I discovered how special southern New Mexico is. Speaking of, a shout out to Milagro Café in Las Cruces and The Bean in Mesilla, where I got some serious writing done, not to mention that beautiful run-down adobe house. Thanks to Burt for the cheap rent, and Ty and Matteo for being cool housemates in the hot southwestern summer months of 2007. Thanks to Carrie Carpenter for another house-sitting gig (every writer should be able to lounge with a laptop on a roof deck overlooking a large body of water, in this case Lake Erie). Thanks also to David Morton, even though you never quite got what I was trying to do with this book (but I forgive you), and Michael Yarbrough for more than ten years of friendship (courtesy of DJK).

Of course, my New York people and places deserve an extra-special thanks. A big kiss to Phil Hopkins—a much more prolific writer than I!—for your friendship and encouragement, and for introducing me to two other quintessential Gen Xers, Jen Bekman and Erin Keating, who shared their stories in *Slackonomics* (not to mention all the other interviewees). Annetta Marion, your determination to attend the AFI directing workshop for women and finish your film inspired me to stick it out with this book. Karlis Rekevics, you are an amazing sculptor and a generous friend. Janet Babin, April Baer, Alex Bandon, Andrew Blum, Seth Brown, Ian Carmody, Cary Conover, Jeremy Cooke, Elizabeth Currid, David Frankel, Dylan Kidd, Jose Lopez, Alex Marshall, Claudia Preparata, Bonnie Remeika, Kovid Saxena, Shin-pei Tsay, Christine Vannoy—all of you are creative forces in your own right. Lorri L., without the sublet on St. Marks Place, this book would not exist. Period. Thanks to a couple of boy toys for taking the edge off—you know who you are! I also have to send big love to Mudspot and crew, the best café in the world, which just happens to be in the best neighborhood in the world: the East Village. More love to Tricia Donegan and the yogis at Bikram Yoga Lower East Side—without ya'll I'm just another failed writer in New York.

I am also grateful to my agent Neil Salkind, who was on the receiving end of more than one temper tantrum. And to Keith Wallman, who saw the potential in my meager book proposal. And to Jonathan Crowe, the final editor of the book, who skillfully pinched-hit in the ninth inning. Thanks to Clair Glass for some research help.

Hugs and kisses for Mom, undoubtedly my most enthusiastic fan, with the possible exception of my dad, who told me long ago, "There's always room at the top." More hugs and kisses for Uncle Goo-Goo and Grandma Hetrick, who helped with financial support at some critical moments, and of course my brother Todd, who taught me how not to throw like a girl.

Last, my love to Alexandros Washburn.

Introduction: Bridging the Analog and Digital Generations

When I first began shopping this book idea around, few publishers were interested unless it contained "good news" or a "self-help" component. At first I tried to play nice, agreeing to team up with a personal financial planner who was going to write sidebars about how to get out of debt, how to invest for the future, etc. (because no one should be taking financial advice from me, that's for sure). But the original proposal didn't sell—thank god. Bookstore shelves are already littered with Suze Orman–like personal finance how-tos for the "young, fabulous and broke." But Generation X is not so young anymore, and when we were, "fabulous" was not cool.

With or without the self-help crap, the book I would have written shortly after having penned an article for the *New York Observer* in January 2004 titled "Generation X: Born Under a Bad Economic Sign," would not have been this one. *Slackonomics* will not argue that our economic situation is worse now than some other time or place, like the Depression. We're living in a totally different world, with different expectations and greater resources than any other country, in a global economy that is infinitely more complex than at any time in history. Comparing one era to another is not only tedious, but also wrongheaded. Claiming that life is so much better now because we've got the Internet, cell phones, digital cameras, and cheap airfare ignores other realities of our current situation, such as job insecurity, income inequality, global warming, and shitty health care.

The premise of *Slackonomics* is that not since the Industrial Revolution has a generation been so whipsawed by the economy, from McJobs to outsourcing, mind-boggling income inequality to two unprecedented back-to-back bubbles (with more to come?). But that isn't the whole story. In this book's subtitle is the phrase "creative destruction," a concept developed by the Austrian economist Joseph Schumpeter* to describe how capitalism renews itself through seemingly sudden economic convulsions. Stagnant industries are destroyed and people get hurt in the churn (think demise of General Motors), while creative ideas and new industries—driven by entrepreneurs—are able to flourish (think Google). This happened during the Industrial Revolution, and it's happening again with the information/technology revolution. Creative Destruction 2.0.

But even that isn't the whole story; it's more like the backstory. What this book is really about is the unique cultural ex-

*Schumpeter (1883–1950) reportedly said he had three aspirations: to be Vienna's best lover, Austria's best horseman, and the world's best economist. He admitted to having trouble with the horses.

perience that comes from living in a time of creative destruction. All the cultural trends, lifestyle choices, and sociological circumstances of the post-boomer generation are being driven by two seemingly contradictory forces that define the current era: economic insecurity on the one hand and the unleashing of human potential as a result of advanced technology on the other. This contradiction has deeply affected everyday life for this generation, ranging from how we work, where we live, how we play, and when we marry and have children, to our attitudes about love, humor, friendship, happiness, and personal fulfillment.

In other words, *Slackonomics* is not an academic white paper; it is written for people who, for example, understand family dynamics from watching *Married With Children* and *The Simpsons*. It is written for women who got in touch with their post-feminist rage through riot grrrl music and *Thelma and Louise*. It is written for people who might have dabbled in Corporate America, but found themselves working at one time or another in an entirely new arena or as free agents without having exactly planned for it. It is written for people who, regardless of whether they have taken a traditional route to marriage, parenthood, and homeownership, still don't exactly feel (or look or act) like "grown-ups." It is written for people with a sense of humor, who long ago developed an appreciation for the absurdity of life. (Pardon me if this is starting to sound like an Internet dating ad.) In other words, this book is a portrait of a generation, not a screed; it is descriptive, not polemical. It is written for people interested in understanding the context that shapes our lives and how this generation will influence the future.

Part of Generation X's story is that the Great Middle Class Squeeze got under way just as we were becoming the middle demographic of the middle class. Not all Xers are in financial dire straits. Hardly. But even people who made practical choices have gone through layoffs and/or career changes, which make it very difficult to plan for—or sometimes even imagine—the future, much less act to change or influence the course of events, both in their own lives and on a larger scale. But despite economic insecurity, or perhaps because of it, this generation has stemmed or reversed just about every bad social trend: (unwanted) unwed birth, suicide, and divorce rates have all declined within this demographic. Generation X is better educated, uses less drugs and alcohol, and is generally healthier and more physically active than previous generations.[1]

Of course, reversing social trends is one thing and redirecting economic forces is another. But Generation X is uniquely positioned to correct the excesses of the baby-boomers by taking a more practical, sustainable approach to the economics of life, be that on a personal, national, or even global scale. Just as this generation is taking on the primary responsibility for paying taxes, setting policy, running businesses and, indeed, the country itself in a globalized world, to hear people discuss the decline of the American empire is not unusual. Whether or not this discussion is a Chicken Little scenario, virtually no one is talking about "Morning in America," and it is the post-boomer generation who will be first in line to deal with this reality. The next twenty years will be crucial for solving huge problems rooted in the fundamental economics of resource allocation.

Fortunately, Gen Xers are not starry-eyed idealists,* but rather steely-eyed realists who could very well be charged with bringing the economy back from the brink. Generation X has always prided itself on being independent of both mind and action, being resistant to conventional wisdom and open to innovation and new ideas that don't conform to any one ideological camp. Xers will have to muster all the mental acuity and ideological flexibility we can to not only wrestle with how we live as individuals but how we will shape the twenty-first century.

Now I'd like to make a few notes about the term "Generation X," which is both more and less than an age group. People who identify with the label (and even those who don't), generally speaking, were born in the mid-1960s through the 1970s, and grew up mostly in middle-class suburbs during the 1980s. (Surprisingly, I discovered that the term is used as much if not more often in Canada, England, Australia, and New Zealand—usually without the scorn and self-loathing.) But Gen X demographics are notoriously fluid. As the Census Bureau puts Xers as those born between 1961 and 1981, other demographers say Gen X was born between 1964 and 1979.

*By "idealists" I mean both the hippy-dippy "peace and love" types and the neoconservative "spreading democracy through the barrel of a gun" variety.

But perhaps Groucho Marx's sentiment sums up the American Gen X attitude best: "I would not join any club that would have someone like me for a member."*

And yet, here we are. Even though the term "Generation X" has been overused and reviled, it still seems to stick. People have tried to rename this generation—without success. In the early 1990s, one author came up with the Free Generation; *New York* magazine tried to coin the term "grups" (because we never seem to grow up). But these terms don't convey anything about the shared cultural experience of this demographic. Like it or not, we're pretty much Generation X for the duration.

So if you know the lyrics, sing along: Xers were the original "latchkey kids." Our mothers went off to work and/or our parents divorced in unprecedented numbers. We ate sugary cereals and watched after-school specials until MTV came along. Extreme sports for most of us meant riding bikes over homemade three-foot ramps without helmets (à la Napoleon Dynamite). Girls renounced bra-burning feminism, there was little awareness of homosexuality among our peers, and although there were the beginnings of hip-hop/rap crossover hits, black and white youth cultures were still pretty distinct and sepa-

*As Chuck Klosterman (a self-described Xer whom people seem to love to hate) wrote in *Sex, Drugs and Cocoa Puffs,* "I know nobody uses the term Generation X anymore, and I know all the people it supposedly describes supposedly hate the supposed designation. But I like it. It's simply the easiest way to categorize a genre of people who . . . share a similar cultural experience. It's not pejorative or complimentary; it's factual. I'm a 'Gen Xer,' okay? And I buy shit marketed to 'Gen Xers.' And I use air quotes when I talk, and I sigh a lot, and I own a Human League cassette. Get over it." (New York: Scribner, 2004: 150.)

rate. We went to college in huge numbers and maybe went on to earn graduate degrees.

We're notoriously disdainful of politics (although that is likely to change in the 2008 election as "anxious Xers" become the new "soccer moms").[2] On the one hand, Xers are practical and cautious; on the other, we have a tendency to roll the dice, which has paid off at times, but other times not so much. We're skeptical, individualistic, and downright distrustful of group-think. We're ambitious rather than careerist, seeking to balance work and family, security and fulfillment.

But most of all, we bridged the analog and digital generations. Some of us didn't touch a computer until college, and few of us grew up on them, but all of us found ourselves on the front lines of the tech revolution and globalization whether we were ready or not.

1

My Future's So Bright, I Gotta Wear Shades

Does it seem like 1980s nostalgia lasted longer than the original era? In many ways it was the perfect decade for the VH1 treatment: there was no all-encompassing, horrifying experience for kids growing up in the 1980s the way World War II or President Kennedy's assassination was for previous generations. There were no bummer social movements spawning marches, protests, and sit-ins. There was no cataclysmic event of 9/11 proportions or the war on terror jolting awake an entire generation in its formative years. The predominant images filtering down from on high—when this demographic was known as the babybusters or boomerangers—came primarily from yuppie culture: Porsches (red 944s); cocaine (the overachiever's drug); blue, pinstriped, double-breasted suits; and career women climbing the corporate ladder in floppy silk bowties.

Self-described socialist and author Barbara Ehrenreich complained about CEOs making a million dollars a year in her 1980s anti-yuppie screed, *Fear of Falling*. But reading it today, you can almost hear Dr. Evil demanding a ransom of "one million dollars!" to much laughter. Now it's hard to understand what all the fuss was about. The ultimate yuppie TV show *Thirtysomething* created some memorably annoying characters, but their nouveau 1980s sophistication consisted of drinking Robert Mondavi wine and living in smallish bungalows in the inner-ring suburbs (kind of the Whopper Junior to today's McMansions).

Compared to where things had been, however, the backlash was on. The counterculture imploded and the mainstream was reasserting itself with a vengeance: anti-hippy, -feminist, -homo—against all identity politics in general—but mostly against the notion of anticonsumerism and antimaterialism. "Get a haircut" and "get a job" were meant to be stinging rejoinders. Thinking globally and acting locally—once a statement for social activism—had become an economic mantra. Charity events of the "Hands Across America/We Are the World" ilk were parodied mercilessly. Earnest was out; cynical was in. It was a whole new era ushered in by Ronald Reagan, elected to office in a landslide by declaring it was "Morning in America" and offering pancakes to Jimmy Carter's oatmeal. Suddenly Alex P. Keaton was going to be a millionaire by the time he was thirty years old, greed was good, and social activism was deader than disco.

The predominant if not always explicit message of the time was that 1960s-era idealism caused the social and economic chaos of the 1970s and should be rejected in favor of narrow self-interest. Social theory justifying selfishness proliferated, most notably with the cooptation of *The Selfish Gene*, a book by evolutionary biologist Richard Dawkins. Published in 1976, it influenced contemporary thinking well beyond evolutionary biology throughout the 1980s. The original premise of *The Selfish Gene* sought in part to explain seemingly altruistic animal behavior as not a consequence of one member of a species helping another survive for the good of the group, but merely the result of genes acting to replicate themselves. In other words, altruism in biology is the economic equivalent of a positive externality.*

"I shall argue," Dawkins writes, "that a predominant quality to be expected in a successful gene is ruthless selfishness."[1] His timing couldn't have been better. Distorted to fit an agenda (the same way Social Darwinism was a misappropriation of natural selection to justify racism and eugenics), the theory became a rationalization for unfettered ambition; never mind that Dawkins also suggested that, because we have consciousness, humans are the only species that can override biological determinism. So the selfish gene theory had mutated from a gene-centric view of evolution to the biological version of laissez-faire economics espoused by Adam Smith, who argued in *The Wealth of Nations* (published in 1776) that although human motives are often selfish and greedy, the competition in the free market would benefit society as a whole.

"By pursuing his own interest he frequently promotes that of society more effectually than when he really intends to promote it. I have never known much good done by those who

---

*An externality is a consequence not reflected in the price of a transaction, which can be either positive or negative (pollution is often cited as a negative externality).

affected to trade for the public good," Smith wrote. Often considered the grandfather of modern economics, Smith enjoyed a cultlike revival in the 1980s and was often cited for his opposition to government protection of markets. What was often overlooked, however, is that (as the Industrial Revolution unleashed unprecedented social ills) Smith advocated for government *intervention* to mitigate the logical extreme of greed and selfishness. He argued that the government had an obligation to prevent humans from veering toward a "vile maxim," which he defined as "All for ourselves, and nothing for other people." But that part of his economic theory didn't fit with the cultural zeitgeist of the 1980s.

It was in this milieu that Gen X came of age. It is no wonder, then, from fictional film characters to pop songs and TV shows, that what were meant to be takedowns and parodies became cultural signposts embraced by this generation. The movie *Wall Street*, released in 1987 and directed by baby-boomer conspiracy theorist Oliver Stone, was meant to be a morality tale between an honorable, hardworking, blue-collar union leader and a predatory, corrupt, and greedy white-collar corporate raider. But despite illegal activities by Gekko, such as insider trading (which, in the post-Enron era of Halliburton, seems very Martha Stewart), the moral of the story has been all but forgotten as it became completely overshadowed by his "greed is good" speech. Ostensibly taken from comments made by real-life corporate raider Ivan Boesky, the mantra took on a life of its own:

> The point is, ladies and gentlemen: Greed, for lack of a better word, is good. Greed works, greed is right. Greed clari-

fies, cuts through, and captures the essence of the evolutionary spirit. Greed in all its forms, greed for life, money, love, knowledge has marked the upward surge in mankind—and greed, you mark my words—will save . . . that other malfunctioning corporation called the USA.

For the post-boomer generation, the cautionary part of the tale just didn't ring true, or at least not as true as "greed is good." Perhaps insider trading wasn't such a great idea, but neither was consigning oneself to a monotonous life of blue-collar work, which was disappearing, anyway. Unions were dead or—worse—corrupt, and regimented manufacturing jobs only led to a stifling life in a cookie-cutter, vinyl-sided clapboard house in suburban dystopia. This disaffection for the collective high road in favor of individual advancement was articulated when the one-hit wonder Timbuk3 scored big in 1986 with the song "The Future's So Bright, I Gotta Wear Shades." The lyrics were meant to be a critique of shallow ambition but, once again, young boomerangers didn't interpret the song that way. Like Gekko's "greed is good" catchphrase, in an act of cultural jujitsu, the song's title was adopted as a badge of honor, allowing yuppie-wannabes to wear ambition on their sleeves. Alex P. Keaton, the young Reagan Republican from the 1980s TV show *Family Ties,* which took place in Columbus, Ohio, was meant to be a somewhat insulting caricature that initially wasn't even supposed to be central to the show and yet ended up defining an era.

Edward Willmott, born in 1964, was raised in the exurbs of Cleveland, Ohio, by middle-class, educated parents who had a nice house on a large lot, two cars, and enough for family vacations, which his parents sometimes took without the kids on their BMW motorcycle. Eddy fully expected to achieve all of that and then some. With a slight build and wisecracking sense of humor, he even looked and sounded a bit like Alex P. Keaton. Eddy too had a passion for economics, liked to make fun of "dance majors," and was a devoted supply-sider and a supporter of Ronald Reagan, which situated him squarely in the "conservative Republican" camp (although he would be considered a moderate by today's standards). By the age of twenty-one, he had leased a chocolate brown Audi and was ready to grab the world by the balls.

So much so that he left college early to work full-time as a salesman for a company that bought, sold, and leased large mainframe computers: the hot new industry. Work was rewarding in ways that school was not. It was fast-paced. It was immediate. Eddy liked being measured by his sales numbers, not by his ability to regurgitate liberal theory claptrap. He knew that if he worked hard and was good at his job, he would make money—a lot of money. He would be a millionaire by the age of thirty. It was all but a given. Except that it didn't quite work out that way.

"By about 1990, I realized that the entire creative output of my life was the recording on my answering machine. I'm not an artsy-fartsy guy, but that bothered me. I didn't feel like there was anything interesting about my life. I was responsible for generating $350,000 of profit a year, but I was just working for somebody else. The guys I knew who had made a lot of money weren't working for someone else. I'd become bored and disillusioned. So when my boss came to me on May 31, 1991—I remember it was a warm, beautiful, sunny Friday—and said, 'How about if we pay you through the summer, but you don't come back?' it was the best day of my life.

"I took off for Europe, backpacking. Then I went back to school. That's when things changed. There was a period of realizing that I didn't have my priorities straight. The Gordon Gekko 'greed is good' motif just didn't work. I ended up not anywhere near where I thought I was going to be: twenty-seven years old, not a millionaire, not anywhere approaching a millionaire. I owned a modest house and collected rent from boarders so I could finish college. So that was good. But I was not going to be making millions on Wall Street. I'm here to make a good living. That goal has never changed, but not to the exclusion of all else in my life. There wasn't a huge epiphany. It wasn't like I was going to throw away all my worldly possessions. I just thought I could be happier if I wasn't sitting in a cubicle, chewing Tums, and panicking about making my numbers."

Not exactly a total meltdown, but for Eddy, it was transformational nonetheless. Had he made the million he set out to acquire, would he have been more satisfied? Probably not. Facing the fact that he would never be a Wall Street tycoon enabled him to make more practical choices—and just might have afforded him a bit more happiness. Recent psychological studies indicate there is no discernable relationship between wealth and happiness, but there is a notable relationship between *expectations* of wealth and happiness (more on this in Chapter 7). In fact, people who live modestly and expect to be okay with what they have are happier than those who have more but worry about not having enough in the future. In other words, the endless pursuit of wealth "is a formula for discontent."[2]

Now the father of two daughters, Eddy runs a home-improvement business and employs a dozen people, which satisfies his entrepreneurial instinct as well as his latent creativity. But lingering expectations and the specter of a lifelong financial struggle still haunt him, even though he has been able to steadily improve his income. When asked to describe their financial situation, he says it is "below average" regardless that his household income is above the national median (the exact midpoint as opposed to the average) of $48,201 in 2006. But is his continued anxiety simply the result of misaligned expectations? Hardly. For someone staring down the high cost of educating his two daughters and the vicissitudes of running a small business that is largely dependent on the real estate market, knowing that your family's income is above the median isn't terribly reassuring when it seems like the rug could get pulled out at any moment.

Indeed, the undercurrent of the selfish, go-go 1980s was only the beginning of a very real fear of falling. The economy was bifurcating, with the professional middle class getting cleaved. On the heels of manufacturing losses came corporate downsizing and a thinning of the ranks. There were inefficiencies in Corporate America that needed correcting—which the early onset of globalization was doing with a vengeance—but that was cold comfort to the increasing number of white-collar workers getting caught on the wrong side of the bottom line. According to one study, managers in the 1980s were more likely to lose their jobs than were other employees, a trend that only accelerated as the decade progressed: the number of displaced managers was 24 percent higher in the second half of the 1980s than in the first half.[3]

So when people like Eddy were first joining the workforce, the postwar expansion of rising wages, job growth, and stability—enjoyed relatively equally at all levels, which kept income inequality in check—was all but over. Of course, to say that the 1980s economy was either "bad" or "good" would be overly simplistic; the economy was becoming increasingly complex and couldn't be described in monolithic terms. Entry-level wages were still pretty decent in the mid-1980s when compared to what was about to come, but clearly, insecurity had become the new economic order in a dramatically shifting landscape.

The *New York Times* reported in 1985 that "this spring's college graduates are facing one of the bleakest job markets in at least two decades." Even more alarmist, the *Los Angeles Times* ran a story on the same topic with the headline "Entry-Level Job Prospects Poorest Since Depression."[4] And this was before the stock market crash of 1987 and the recession of the early 1990s that really hampered recent college graduates' job prospects. How bad things were for entry-level job-seekers at the time is open to debate, but the nature of work was undergoing a major readjustment. For the first time in the post–World War II era, you could no longer expect to get a job at a company, work your way up over the years, and retire with a decent pension—hardly news today, but quite a shock at the time.

So how to explain the interminable 1980s nostalgia? Not surprisingly, it didn't much focus on declining economic fortunes or yuppie culture, but rather on New Wave haircuts, Madonna wannabes, Chucky the horror movie doll, and parachute pants. VH1 gave everyone permission to shamelessly rock out to music that had long since been declared an embarrassment of the era: Pat Benatar, Duran Duran, and don't forget Mötley Crüe, dude! Once the music (and the irony) subsided, you could even engage in a little intellectual discourse about the significance that the Crüe actually had. "Seriously, they were like a huge influence on the Chili Peppers and Green Day." In many ways it really was a simpler time, but that doesn't mean we all want to forever relive it like a Dennis Hopper retirement plan commercial.

As Michael Hirschorn, executive vice president of programming for VH1, told the *New York Times* in a 2005 piece titled "We Hate the 1980s": "The 80's nostalgia boom is real, but it's not broad. . . . For this group of people, you can't give them straight nostalgia of the sort of baby-boomer, 'everything was wonderful and great when we were kids' feel. People . . . know that things weren't that great. We never thought that Mötley Crüe was saving the world. We identify with them passionately, but with a certain wink."[5]

We might have winked at the Crüe, but I'm not so sure they were winking back. Since releasing albums like *Girls, Girls, Girls*, and *Dr. Feelgood* throughout the 1980s, the band had sobered up and seemed to be taking things pretty seriously, even releasing a sixth album in 1991 titled *Decade of Deca-*

dence. This was followed in 1997 with *Generation Swine*, which depicted a bunch of pigs in yuppie suits on the cover.

In the VH1 version of the 1980s, greed was good, but in reality it was more like a necessary evil. Throw in a little youthful bravado and some cognitive dissonance, and—voilà—you've got Alex P. Keaton and real-life counterparts like Eddy Willmott: garden-variety suburban kids from Middle America, 500 miles from Wall Street, aspiring to be Masters of the Universe. It is no wonder then that the first wave of post-boomers—who largely do not identify with the term "Generation X"—feel they were led astray by 1980s yuppie culture that wasn't really of their own making.

2

The Outliers

What does the novel *Generation X* have in common with the TV show *Melrose Place*? It's not the typical question that an economist would ask, but I'm not an economist (not even a "rogue" one) and this isn't a textbook. It's Slackonomics.

At first glance, the saucy nighttime soap wouldn't seem to have much in common with *Generation X*, the book that, for better or worse, gave this generation its label and identity, thanks to author Douglas Coupland, who wrote perhaps the last truly defining sociocultural novel before the fragmentation and proliferation of media rendered such a notion obsolete. Published in 1991, it had an incredibly prescient subtitle: *Tales for an Accelerated Culture*.

The long-running Fox hit, on the other hand, is remembered as *Dynasty* transported to Los Angeles circa 1996 rather than the angst-ridden Gen X show that it started out to be. Before Heather Locklear lathered things up, the show centered on a multi-culti group of twentysomethings who lived together in a shabby chic apartment complex where a mix of cynicism, naïveté, ambition, and world-weariness swam together in the shared pool at the center of the action. All the young characters were struggling to realize their creative dreams and pay the rent without compromising their souls.

The very first episode, titled "Sex, Lies and Melrose Place" (edgy!), features Allison Parker (Courtney Thorne-Smith) freaking out because her roommate splits in the middle of the night, sticking her with the entire month's rent, due in a matter of days—which of course she does not have. In a panic, she knocks on the door of the apartment manager, a young, somewhat jaded emergency room doctor, Michael Mancini, and begs him to stall the landlord for a few days.

"Stall? Allison, this is real life, you can't stall on the rent," Michael chastises her.

"I finally got a job after three months," Allison whines. "My savings are gone. I'm living on Cup-O-Soup. I just don't have it. This is the worst thing that's ever happened to me!" Hearing her own annoying voice, Allison finally concedes, "I'm an adult and I'm going to have to deal with it." She drives to her job as a lowly receptionist at an advertising agency while circling newspaper roommate ads on the steering wheel of what looks like a dumpy Ford Escort.

By the end of the first episode, Billy Campbell (Andrew Shue)—perhaps the first character on primetime TV to depict a Sensitive New Age Guy, otherwise known as a SNAG—becomes Allison's roommate, fitting right in with the cadre of struggling young creative types. He's an aspiring novelist ("like Norman Mailer," he explains earnestly) and pays the bills by teaching dance at Arthur Murray (which he quits in the second episode to drive a cab). There are hints of the melodrama the show would later become, but by and large the first season centers on the tough choices these characters have to make as they enter the big, scary world of adulthood.

In one episode, a high-level advertising executive sexually harasses Allison. Like Anita Hill, she has to decide whether to stand her ground and risk humiliation, or shut up and swallow her pride. Another character, Jake Hanson (Grant Show), struggles with underemployment at a minimum-wage job at a "trendy" cappuccino joint where he's dumped on by the yuppie customers and humiliated by his boss before quitting in a huff. Rhonda is an African American funk-aerobics instructor who wants to join a serious dance company but isn't sure the sacrifices (both physical and financial) are worth it. In another episode, Billy, who is struggling with his writing career, goes to work for his father at the family-owned furniture store. But when a bitchy customer insults Billy by suggesting he'll say anything to sell her a couch, he quits. A dream deferred for a paycheck is one thing, but not at the expense of his integrity, too. Needless to say, with characters and plotlines hitting a little too close to home, the ratings for the first season were in the toilet. Who wants to watch their own sucky life dramatized on TV, even if every episode ended with a pool party?

Phil Hopkins certainly didn't need to watch Billy Campbell struggle as a writer: he already *was* a struggling writer. Originally from Dallas, Hopkins's father was a public relations executive and his mother a homemaker. He went to college in southern California, eventually graduating from UCLA after six years with a degree in English in 1992, the year *Melrose Place* debuted. This was also the height of the early 1990s recession, which in California was particularly deep. Unable to get a "real" job with his English degree, Hopkins finally got a gig testing video games such as "Zombie Dinos from the Planet Zeltoid," which was described in an old product catalog found on the Internet as "Join wise-cracking Dexter the Dinodroid in his momentous quest. Free the innocent dinosaurs who have become mindless zombies, controlled by the evil Harry the Harriet and his alien Brain Blobs. Travel back 200 million years in Dexter's incredible Time Machine to save the planet and 'kick some brain!'"

"By today's standards, it would look absurd," says Hopkins, who now lives and works in Brooklyn, managing a group of software testers, all of whom live in India, while he writes plays and novels in the evenings. "We were practically encouraged to come to work stoned, all the better to test under realistic conditions. There were about seventy of us in cubicles on one floor of a large office. They let us turn off the lights. Some people actually smoked pot at their desks. There was no adult supervision. People were goofing around, flirting with each other. Everyone was basically the same age, white suburban kids who had just graduated from college.

"I was living in Westwood, near the UCLA campus, paying $475 in rent and I was only making $600 a month. I was taking the Santa Monica bus, about an hour-and-a-half trip, and it only ran every forty minutes. That lasted about a year until everyone got laid off en masse. Someone we had never seen before brought everyone into a conference room and said, 'Thanks for your service, but we no longer require it. Pick up your check on the way out.' No one even asked why. Everyone kind of shrugged and filed out.

"I didn't pay rent for a couple months and everyone else in the apartment was unemployed so we got an eviction notice. Around this time, a friend of mine decided he wanted to move [from Los Angeles] to New York, and I said I was moving back to Texas with my parents because I didn't know what else to do. But first I decided to drive to New York with him.

"The family whose car we drove—they put an ad in the school newspaper for someone to drive their car from LA to Boston—gave us the keys to their car and $200 for gas and that's all the money we had, no credit cards, either. So we split the money and stopped in Vegas, and I put half of mine on black. I'm not making this up. I put $50 down on black and made $200. So we proceeded to New York. I dropped off my friend and he got an apartment while I drove to Boston and returned to New York on the bus. He got a room at an SRO [single room occupancy] with a shared bath for $300 on the Upper West Side. This was early 1994. I stayed there for a week. There were roaches everywhere. That's what you had to do if you wanted to live on your own without help from your parents. I just couldn't do it anymore.

"After a week in New York, I moved back to Dallas with my parents. I had been undereating for so long that I went from 160 to 190 pounds in a month. I went to work for my dad for a year. He was nice about it, but I was humiliated. I felt like a failure. I gained some skills, but I didn't want to follow in my dad's footsteps. I saw how much his job made him miserable and I didn't want to be miserable. He made a living telling lies for big corporations. He spun it, but underneath, he hated it. This is what I was confronting at the age of twenty-six."

Which is precisely what the characters in the first season of *Melrose Place* as well as those in the novel *Generation X* were confronting. In the novel, set in Palm Springs, California, a trio of young, overeducated, underemployed, middle-class twenty-somethings work at "McJobs" and live in run-down bungalows (which they undoubtedly could not afford today). They hang out in the desert (a bereft setting for bereft characters), telling each other stories and trying to make sense of their ennui and disaffection. The book became known less for its plotline and character development than for its neologisms, which are peppered throughout the margins of the book, many as relevant today as ever, such as Option Paralysis: "The tendency, when given unlimited choices, to make none,"[1] a phenomenon also written about in 2005 by Barry Schwartz, a professor of social theory at Swarthmore College, in *The Paradox of Choice: Why More Is Less.** Other examples include:

Voter Block: The attempt, however futile, to register dissent with the current political system by simply not voting.

Lessness: A philosophy whereby one reconciles oneself with diminished expectations of material wealth. "I've

---

*Through experiments and argumentation, Schwartz shows that the more choices people have, the more bewildered they become and the less able they are to make a selection, and, even when they do, they tend to feel less satisfied about their choice. (New York: HarperCollins, 2004.)

given up wanting to make a killing or be a bigshot. I just want to find happiness."

Yuppie Wannabe's: An X generation subgroup that believes the myth of a yuppie life-style as being both satisfying and viable. Tend to be highly in debt, involved in some form of substance abuse, and show a willingness to talk about Armageddon after three drinks.[2]

In fact, the book was originally conceived as a Preppy Handbook–type guide to Generation X. But that is not to dismiss it as lightweight (which some overstuffed critics invariably did). Succinct and engaging, it was perhaps just a little too readable for critical acclaim (which was more generous in hindsight). But Coupland didn't just coin catchy buzzwords. He also predicted the future in the way only an artist can, so aptly put by Marshall McLuhan: "The artist is the only person; his antennae pick up these messages before anybody. So he is always thought of as being way ahead of his time because he lives in the present."[3]

Coupland was clearly influenced by Marshall McLuhan, a Canadian professor and communications theorist who was an early pioneer of pop culture analysis and incredibly prescient about the coming technological revolution. In 1959 McLuhan delivered a lecture about the revolutionary effects of electronic media, in which he said, "Taken in the long run, the medium is the message. So that when, by group action, a society evolves a new medium like print or telegraph, or photo or radio, it has earned the right to express a new message. And when we tell the young that this new message is a threat to the old message or medium . . . the young can only conclude that we are not serious. And this is the meaning of their decline of attention."[4]

McLuhan himself became a pop culture icon, culminating with a cameo in Woody Allen's film *Annie Hall*. In a twist of irony, by the end of his long and influential career, he suffered from overexposure, and his ideas had lost their currency when he died in 1980;[5] that is, until he was rediscovered fifteen years after his death by Silicon Valley techies for his prediction that one day we would learn via an "electronic circuitry system," which he made thirty years before the Internet revolution.

Much like McLuhan's predictions, when Coupland's book arrived on the scene, just how accelerated the culture would become as a result of the technological revolution wasn't yet fully appreciated. The fragmentation of media into tiny bits had only begun to smash the old message like a particle accelerator, breaking it down while at the same time revealing its properties. The speed and volume of media were about to increase to the point where it could only be consumed horizontally rather than vertically. Vertical media consumption might be thought of as watching TV and seeing different representations in a single format (car commercial, public service message, *Little House on the Prairie, Saturday Night Live*), while horizontal consumption of media is absorbing content of a similar sensibility across different formats, like geological strata that reveal conditions of a certain era around the earth. It is precisely at the beginning of this phenomenon when Coupland's book was published, which was just a few months ahead of Richard Linklater's movie *Slacker* (July 1991), followed quickly by Nirvana's *Nevermind* (September 1991)—a trifecta of culturally defining works of similar sensibility across three different media. Slackonomics, it would seem, was born in a very spontaneous, meme-like fashion.*

All three of these works had a similar message despite their different media: diminished expectations had become the defining force for this post-hippy, post-punk generation for whom both the idealist and the nihilist were oversimplified, pathetic characters. Gen Xers had spent four years in college watching the economic shit hit the fan (or longer—the time it took to complete a bachelor's degree was lengthening due to the increasing cost of college and a decreasing sense of urgency about reaching adulthood). Graduating into a terrible recession made the late '80s job market look flush by comparison. Given these circumstances, the slacker phenomenon is all too easily explained as defensive posturing in reaction to a lack of opportunity. And this, of course, presented the prescient artist with a cultural moment ripe for a new anti-manifesto kind of manifesto.

"Hey, I may live badly, but at least I don't have to work hard to do it." This is one of the enduring lines from *Slacker*, Richard Linklater's film that follows young bohemian characters living in Austin, Texas, as they encounter each other in a successive chain link throughout the day. Having been weaned on TV, these post-boomer kids were already considered a

---

*Evolutionary biologist Richard Dawkins, mentioned in Chapter 1, also introduced the term "meme" in his book *The Selfish Gene*, defining it as a method of cultural evolution, the process by which ideas are transmitted and replicated from mind to mind.

media-saturated lot, but they were also a very educated demographic. These alterna-philosophers reveled in the art of deconstructing everything from the assassination of JFK to a deeper meaning of the Smurfs. Whether these characters were underachievers or economically frustrated (or a combination thereof) was not necessarily the point. Nonetheless, they were young adults not born rich enough to spend a few post-college years hanging out in Europe sipping wine before joining Daddy's firm, but were too smart and savvy to be satisfied with service sector or blue-collar work. Options, needless to say, were limited. Or perhaps there were too many, none particularly more desirable than another, leading to option paralysis.

According to the Economic Policy Institute, a liberal think tank in Washington, D.C., the average wage offers of newly hired college graduates crested in 1985, stagnated for several years, then dropped precipitously in the early 1990s. Entry-level wages didn't rebound to the 1985 level until as late as 1999. In other words, it took an unprecedented bubble economy to boost entry-level wages back to where they had been in the mid-1980s.

Hard times for everyone, right? Not necessarily. At the same time wages for newly minted graduates were dropping, income inequality was increasing. Beginning in 1980, the story of increasing income inequality is partly the result of a growing generational wealth gap. According to Census Bureau data, the median income of young workers as a percentage of those aged forty-five to fifty-four dropped significantly between 1980 and 1990. In 1980, men between the ages of twenty and twenty-four earned 55 percent of what older men made. In 1990, that percentage dropped to 35 percent. A similar drop occurred for women. In 1980, twenty- to twenty-four-year-old women earned almost 80 percent of what forty-five- to fifty-four-year-olds earned. By 1990, that dropped to less than 60 percent.[6]

Income inequality, or the gap between the haves and have-nots, is of course an old one. What's remarkable, however, is that in the twenty-first century it continues unabated to the point that there is now a growing rift between the relatively well-off and the super-rich. Between 1949 and 1979, income at all levels grew relatively equally, but since then income growth has occurred disproportionately at the upper echelons. The richest 1 percent increased their portion of the national income from 8.2 percent in 1980 to 17.4 percent in 2005.[7] By another measure, the top 1 percent saw their wealth increase by 42 percent between 1983 and 1998, almost four times the gain of the middle 20 percent.[8] The Economic Policy Institute calculated that in 2004 only the top 5 percent of households increased their incomes, while the remaining 95 percent had flat or falling incomes.[9]

By 2006, according to Census Bureau data, the top 300,000 earners raked in almost as much income as the bottom *150 million*.[10]

So what? you ask. It's not just that asymmetrical income distribution is unfair and breeds resentment, it's actually bad for the economy, dampening productivity, contributing to ill health, fostering corruption, and encouraging waste. Worse, it becomes self-perpetuating.[11] It's also largely the result of policy choices made by older generations that have been foisted on Gen X, who will pay the price in the short term and—without major changes—well into the future.*

It's no wonder then that *Melrose Place*, which started out as a realistic depiction (relatively speaking) of Gen X, post-college angst about how to earn a living without selling your soul, got bad ratings until it morphed into a sublimely stupid nighttime soap in pencil skirts and heels. As *New Yorker* writer Malcolm Gladwell noted on the eve of the show's final episode in 1999: "In the mid-nineteen-nineties, when a generation of Americans reached adulthood and suddenly realized that they didn't want to be there, the inverted world of Melrose was a wonderfully soothing place. Here, after all, was a show that ostensibly depicted sophisticated grownup society, and every viewer was smarter than the people on the screen."

*One suggestion for stemming the ever-widening gap between the haves and have-nots is a progressive consumption tax, as proposed by Cornell University economist Robert Frank, in his book *Falling Behind: How Rising Inequality Harms the Middle Class.*

3

Cunt

The riot grrrl music scene had been simmering underground in the early 1990s about the same time that Seattle boys had reclaimed rock from hair metal purgatory. Bands like Bikini Kill and Bratmobile greased the skids for a mainstream version of the "angry white female," which went mainstream with the biggest-selling album by a female singer ever, Alanis Morissette's *Jagged Little Pill*. Her lyrics crackled with the post-feminist rage of someone who had grown up during the backlash 1980s when self-respecting girls had no problem giving head but denied being feminists despite (1) agreeing with nearly every feminist principle, such as equal pay for equal work, and (2) benefiting greatly from the road to equality that was being paved ahead of them by "bra burners" and other hairy-legged types who ostensibly hated sex and men. Alanis Morissette's rage against The Man was not about an oppressive patriarchy trying to *keep* her down, but about a cheating boyfriend who didn't appreciate it when she *went* down: "An older version of me, is she perverted like me, would she go down on you in a theater?"

For young girls, being called a "women's libber" on the 1980s playground was more insulting than being called a slut. As Susan Faludi exhaustively documented in her 1991 best-selling book, *Backlash: The Undeclared War Against American Women* (a rather overheated subtitle, but nonetheless . . .), popular culture throughout the 1980s was rife with the message that it in fact was too much education and financial independence that were causing women so much misery, drastically reducing their chances for marriage, causing infertility, and, for older women, leading to divorce and heartbreak.

The culmination of this "backlash" occurred in 1986—just as straight, pubescent Gen X girls were discovering boys—when *Newsweek* (among many other publications relying on a dubious, unpublished study by a Yale sociologist and a Harvard economist) declared that by age forty, a single, educated career woman is more likely to be "killed by a terrorist" than to ever get married. The study concluded, "white, college-educated women born in the mid-1950s who are still single at 30 have only a 20 percent chance of marrying. By the age of 35 the odds drop to 5 percent."[1] As Mark Twain once said, a lie can get halfway around the world before the truth gets its boots on—and that was long before (Al Gore supposedly invented)* the Internet.

*One more time for the record, Gore never said he "invented" the Internet. He told CNN on March 9, 1999, "During my service in the United States Congress, I took the initiative in creating the Internet." Many sources give credit to Gore for recognizing the potential of high-speed national networking as far back as the 1970s, which he began promoting as an "information super highway" in the 1980s, and introduced legislation in the late 1980s and early 1990s to fund its development.

Having come of age at a time of widespread antipathy toward "feminism," a new perspective began to take shape among young Gen X women that seemed to flip the original feminist slogan on its head: the personal wasn't political; the political had become personal. Old school feminism had sought equality via government intervention, and despite some notable successes (such as Title IX, which required equal funding in schools for female activities, which led to the sports revolution for young women), the Equal Rights Amendment to the Constitution failed twice. One could argue, though, that the opportunity to play and excel at sports would have a more profound effect on individual girls and their sense of "empowerment" than an amendment to the Constitution conferring an abstract notion of equality, which didn't even address the issue of economic parity.* In other words, government action isn't meaningless when enforceable laws have a specific and tangible effect on the daily lives of individuals.

And that is precisely how Gen X women repurposed feminism, even if they dropped the term itself, which had become loaded with negative connotations: "Post-feminism assumes . . . that now it is up to individual women to make personal choices that simply reinforce those fundamental societal changes. Put this way, 'feminist' practices become matters of personal style or individual choice and any emphasis on organized intervention is regarded as naïve."[2]

---

*The entire text of the ERA reads: "Section 1. Equality of rights under the law shall not be denied or abridged by the United States or by any state on account of sex. Section 2. The Congress shall have the power to enforce, by appropriate legislation, the provisions of this article. Section 3. This amendment shall take effect two years after the date of ratification."

Boomer feminists accuse Xers of having no idea what it used to be like, taking everything they achieved for granted, having a sense of entitlement. All true. But frankly, girls *should* take equality for granted. As for Xers, they concluded that old school feminism had become too rigid, denied women the right to be attractive and feminine, was hopelessly unrealistic about biological differences, and completely lacked a sense of humor. The notion that "a woman needs a man like a fish needs a bicycle" rang as false as *Wall Street*'s morality tale of the noble blue-collar union leader versus the evil corporate raider.

The baby-boomer dismissal of "Third Wave" feminism* is a failure to understand the different economic realities in which these two generations came of age. After all, Xers were the first generation of girls to grow up assuming they would have a career and make their own money, partly out of a desire for professional fulfillment, but also out of sheer necessity. Having witnessed the struggle that some older women experienced as a result of demanding independence but often not having the economic wherewithal to sustain it, Gen X girls were instilled with a sense that to rely on men was downright foolish. On the other hand, not having a man could result in a lifetime of struggle, as opportunities were still significantly limited by the proverbial "glass ceiling" as well as a persistent disparity in wages earned by men and women.* In light of this mixed message, it's no wonder that

---

*The movement to gain the right to vote is considered the First Wave. The ERA movement is considered the Second Wave, closely followed by the Third Wave, which came about as a reaction to both the Second Wave and the 1980s backlash.

female Xers ditched the consciousness-raising sessions and "take back the night" marches in favor of getting educated, developing marketable skills, and entering the workforce en masse, all the while trying to be attractive and sexy.

Growing up in small-town Ohio, Lyz Bly saw her family's secure middle-class lifestyle take a nosedive when her parents divorced. At the age of twelve, she and her younger brother went from enjoying an idyllic childhood playing in the woods behind their spacious three-bedroom house to being cramped in a basement apartment in a shabby rental complex. Their lives eventually stabilized after their mother remarried, but seared into Lyz's consciousness was the double-edged lesson that financial independence was necessary for survival, yet having a man meant stability and even prosperity. For Bly and many other young women growing up during the 1980s, this betwixt-and-between conundrum resulted in a kind of repressed feminist anger.

"I remember going to punk shows in the '80s and getting pushed off the dance floor by the guys who were in the mosh pit essentially beating each other up. That was not the place for me. I could identify with the anger, but felt like I couldn't even vent that anger because it was a guys' arena."

As an undergraduate at Kent State University in the late 1980s, Bly remembers hating women and having only male friends, yet

---

*Census data indicate that since 2000, young women in large metropolitan areas earn higher wages than their male counterparts. It remains to be seen if this will even out or reverse as both genders work their way up the professional ladder. ("For Young Earners in Big Cities, A Gap in Women's Favor," *New York Times*, August 3, 2007.)

majoring in fashion design. "I had this white cotton Norma Kamali dress with enormous shoulder pads, the size of a football player; talk about appropriating masculinity." Bly switched to art history ("I got sick of being around girls who just wanted to shop"), eventually earning a master's degree in 1993 from Ohio State University. While she was in graduate school, she got pregnant by her boyfriend at a time when the relationship was already deteriorating. Not wanting to have an abortion, however, they decided the best thing to do was get married ("As a feminist, I am pro-choice, but I just wouldn't choose that for myself"). Unfortunately, the marriage only lasted about a year, and Bly was stunned to find herself an overeducated single mother looking for work at a very inopportune time.

"I took a job at Borders Books in Westlake [a suburb of Cleveland], which had just opened. It was a haven for people who were intelligent and had degrees but couldn't find jobs. I remember getting offered the community relations position and they said, 'You're going to like the salary, it's $17,000.' I was like, 'Are you kidding?' But they had health insurance and I didn't have any other offers, so I took it. So I'm hanging out at Borders with other white, suburban middle-class kids who couldn't find jobs, and we all started sharing music. The café manager and I were really into riot grrrl stuff. So we'd order Bikini Kill and other stuff that you couldn't get anywhere else then.

"At this point, I was completely immersed in the music to find a voice for my brand of feminism," continues Bly, who is remarried and is now earning a PhD in gender and culture studies, and recently adopted a girl from Guatemala. "This is hard to articulate exactly, but there was this feeling of wanting to embrace girlie things that my mother's generation had eschewed, like knitting and sewing. I had grown up with the idea that the way to prison as a woman was to stay home and cook and clean and sew. So we went toward this professional life, and then to be faced with the fact that I couldn't find a job and pay my bills after getting a master's degree—it was very disillusioning. It makes you feel like you aren't an adult. There was this moment when we embraced the little girl aesthetic, Hello Kitty and stuff like that. When we were kids we were told that being a girl wasn't good because that's not how you make it in the world, but then we get out in the world and not being able to make it on our own, and having to depend on our parents, even when I was a parent—that's what kind of sparked the anger. So the riot grrrl scene came along, with lyrics like, 'white boy, don't laugh, don't cry, just die,' and Kathleen Hanna was singing it in a miniskirt and tattoos. It was this huge release valve."

At the same time that Hanna of Bikini Kill was singing "White Boy: Don't laugh, don't cry, just die" in a miniskirt and tattoos, she was also writing song lyrics such as "I Like Fucking: . . . I believe in the radical possibilities of pleasure, babe / I do, I do, I do"—an aggressive, contemporary version of Molly Bloom's soliloquy at the end of James Joyce's *Ulysses*: "yes I said yes I will Yes." Embracing aggressive sexuality served the dual purpose of rebelling against the Andrea Dworkins* of the previous generation as well as acknowledging the reality that sexual

*Dworkin was a radical feminist and lawyer who crusaded against pornography and even argued that all sexual relationships between men and women were inherently oppressive in a patriarchal society.

appeal can be powerful—and to deny that or to give that power away is cutting off your nose to spite your face.

So while images of working women in the 1980s looked like desexualized playboy bunnies, à la Melanie Griffith in *Working Girl*, young professional women by the late 1990s were depicted in micro-miniskirts, à la Ally McBeal. This of course sparked cries of sexism from old school feminists who objected to McBeal's hand-wringing about being single, her seeming lack of professionalism, and her emotional instability. But the show was a huge hit, in no small part due to its relevance to Gen X women, who related to feeling pulled in all directions. The McBeal phenomenon reached its apex when *Time* magazine infamously juxtaposed Susan B. Anthony, Betty Friedan, and Gloria Steinem with McBeal and asked, "Is Feminism Dead?"[3] In fact, old school feminism *was* dead, and it had been for at least fifteen years when *Time* posed the question.

What *Time* magazine should have asked is, "What's *Really* Bugging Ally McBeal?" Maybe it's that no matter how short the skirt or how fancy the degree, McBeal only made about seventy-five cents for every dollar her male colleagues earned. Although women have made enormous professional strides, the wage gap between men and women for this generation has remained stubbornly persistent. In fact, throughout the 1980s, when the wage gap seemed to be narrowing, it turned out to be as much the result of men's wages dropping as women's wages rising. According to a report issued in 2003 by the General Accounting Office (renamed the Government Accountability Office), "even accounting for factors such as occupation, industry, race, marital status and job tenure . . . working women today earn an average of 80 cents for every dollar earned by their male counterparts. This pay gap has persisted for the past two decades, remaining relatively consistent from 1983–2000."[4] Since then, things have gotten worse.

One reason for this may be that with every recession, the wage gap increases again, and the most recent recession was no different. By 2003 women's wages had dropped back to seventy-five cents on the dollar. "Between 2002 and 2003, median annual earnings for full-time year-round women workers shrank by 0.6 percent, to $30,724, while men's earnings remained unchanged, at $40,668. The 1.4 percent decrease in the gender wage ratio is the largest backslide in 12 years (since 1991). The 2003 Census data also show the first decline in women's real earnings since 1995."[5] More recent data are even worse. In 2005, "college-educated women between 36 and 45 years old earned 74.7 cents in hourly pay for every dollar that men in the same group did, according to Labor Department data analyzed by the Economic Policy Institute. A decade earlier, the women earned 75.7 cents."[6]

One subtle but not terribly surprising reason for the persistent wage gap is the problem of unconscious bias. Studies have shown that once gender is neutralized, women achieve at much higher rates. For instance, when orchestras began conducting "blind" auditions, where candidates performed behind a screen, "the percentage of women hired by the top five U.S. orchestras has risen from less than five percent to 34 percent."[7] But of course, Ally McBeal, in her quest to become partner at the law firm, can't audition behind a screen. So she might as well show a little leg. Couldn't hurt. Might help.

Another possible reason for the never-ending wage gap, as cited by the GAO study, is the perception that men are still the primary providers while women who are mothers are not productive workers. Men with children earn 2.1 percent more than men without children, while women with children earn 2.5 percent *less* than women without children. It's no wonder then that Gen X women—despite having been subjected to *Newsweek*'s "marriage crunch" scare at a formative age—are marrying and having children later in life than boomer women, a fact that was belatedly noted by *Newsweek*.

It took twenty years for the magazine to retract its controversial cover story, but better late than never. On May 31, 2006, *Newsweek* admitted to knowing soon after printing that single, educated, forty-year-old women are "more likely to be killed by a terrorist" than to ever get married that it was based on an unpublished study using numbers that were way off base. The magazine admitted, "Months later, other demographers came out with new estimates suggesting a 40-year-old woman really had a 23 percent chance of marrying. Today, some researchers put the odds at more than 40 percent. Nevertheless, it quickly became entrenched in pop culture (probably because *Newsweek* failed to report a correction)." *Newsweek* was able to relocate eleven of the fourteen women interviewed for the original article, and "among them, eight ended up marrying, and three remain single. Several had children. None divorced."[8]

As Alanis Morissette might ask, "Isn't it ironic?"*

---

*Alanis Morissette's lyrics for the song "Ironic" are a case study in irony. Every scenario she sings about as an example of irony are in fact not irony at all, but more like Murphy's Law—which is the real irony. But I digress.

4

I'm a Loser, Baby, So Why Don't You Pay Me

Undoubtedly there are lots of people born roughly between 1963 and 1977 who are perfectly satisfied working a traditional job in Corporate America. They are probably not reading this book. The inability to get a foothold on the corporate ladder at a formative age surely had a profound effect on the professional lives of many would-be Masters of the Universe (the upside of which would be averting the inevitable midlife crisis of yore). But plenty of smart and ambitious people—artists and nonartists alike—never really considered Corporate America as a career option, nor did they attempt to take a traditional career path.

Lloyd Dobler pretty well summed up this sentiment in *Say Anything*, the 1989 coming-of-age romantic comedy written and directed by Cameron Crowe. Upon meeting the overprotective father of his love interest, Dobler doesn't exactly live up to the high expectations Daddy has for his overachieving daughter. After hemming and hawing, Dobler finally gives in to a dinner-table grilling about his own professional future by articulating what he doesn't want to do: "I don't want to sell anything, buy anything, or process anything as a career. I don't want to sell anything bought or processed, or buy anything sold or processed, or process anything sold, bought, or processed, or repair anything sold, bought, or processed. You know, as a career, I don't want to do that."

So what *does* Lloyd Dobler want to be when he grows up? Well, he's not sure, but he likes kickboxing: "I think it's got a future," he says jauntily. In comparison to the girl he is courting—and in the context of the late 1980s—having not decided on a career, Dobler represents the underachiever. But he has only recently graduated from high school, after all, and just because he doesn't aspire to a traditional career, how much of a loser could he really be when he pursues the school valedictorian with such confidence and determination? One can imagine him a dozen years later successfully running Dobler's Kickass Kickboxing Gym, which he eventually sells in order to spend more time at home with the kids and try his hand at screenwriting.

According to recent studies, people have a tendency to "know" things intuitively before they actually have the evidence to support their conclusions,[1] and this seems to be true of an entire generation with regard to its economic future. As Jacob Hacker documents in *The Great Risk Shift*, economic instability had been relatively manageable since the Depression until it slowly began ticking upward in the 1980s before rising dramatically in the early 1990s and continuing to climb. In 1970 the chances of experiencing a 50 percent or greater income drop were about 7 percent. By 1992, that risk had reached 17 percent and is still rising. Workers in their *prime earning years* in the 1960s had a 13 percent chance of experiencing a year in poverty; by the 1990s, that had risen to a 36 percent chance.[2] Hacker points out that economic volatility (how much a family's income fluctuates) has risen much faster than income inequality.*

Of course, Corporate America was never a safe haven for whole segments of the population, such as blacks and women, and even though it has become more diverse and dynamic, it has also become increasingly hypercompetitive and fundamentally insecure. For Gen X, without the safety that a traditional career once offered, a distinction began to be made between careerism and ambition, the former associated with soul-sucking cubicle jobs of a highly uncertain future and the latter rooted in a sense of personal fulfillment (and if you're really lucky, meaningful contribution). Having grown up in the era of "Free to Be You and Me," individuality turned out to actually be a detriment in the corporate workplace. So if a traditional career wasn't minimally satisfying or did not provide security, what was the point? Like the forest fires that burned Yellowstone National Park in 1988, globalization was incinerating America's old

---

*Typical of academic warring, a whole debate rages between economists regarding Hacker's conclusions. Suffice it to say—despite a lot of numbers being thrown around—the arguments fall along ideological lines, with the libertarian crowd debunking Hacker's work and the progressive economists supporting it. You know the saying: lies, damn lies, and statistics.

economy, which—while incredibly damaging and disruptive—released a burst of entrepreneurial energy of surprising diversity, even if it wasn't immediately obvious above the level of underbrush.

So despite the admonition to get a "real" job, what were once considered hobbies and/or ill-considered creative pursuits almost accidentally became professional ventures, thereby blurring the sharp lines that had once delineated art and commerce, career and hobby, professional and amateur. From kickboxers to musicians to knowledge workers, more often than not the idea of forging a new path wasn't born out of either a false sense of creative purity or single-minded greed, but rather a combination of desire and necessity. Indeed, rarely was "forging a new path" even the goal. It was simply a matter of doing something enjoyable and seeing what happened next. The trade-off between that and getting a "real job" had become negligible enough to entice a whole lot of people off the traditional career path. These are the economic circumstances that gave rise to what became known as "alternative" culture.

Before "alternative" became a meaningless and overused word, it had gained currency in the 1990s because it applied to a lot more than a new subgenre of rock-and-roll. As one "alternative" publication, *The Baffler*, founded in 1988, describes its origins: "To put it simply, we believed in small magazines and in self-publishing because we had to. Until a certain species of cynicism became acceptable in the mainstream press a few years ago, almost nobody else would publish us. We have been outsiders to the mainstream of our time not merely as a matter of choice, but because . . . the way we thought and wrote about culture was not something encouraged warmly by editors."*

Anything and everything described as alternative, from weekly papers to music to comedy to business plans, had one thing in common: it was cultured in the agar of outsiderness, which in the early Gen X era was synonymous with "loser." Growing up in the 1980s, it seemed anyone who didn't aspire to business school, law school, or medicine was destined for mediocrity, which condemned a whole lot of people to life as an outlier. This was not because of some kind of personality disorder or bohemian sensibility, but rather because what were "mainstream" and its equal opposite (beatnik, hippy) were so narrowly defined that they excluded a whole lot of smart, creative, and ambitious people. So how to forge ahead in this brave new world? Like Dobler, who the hell really knew? Might as well go to the gym and practice some kick-boxing moves.

The image of Gen Xer as loser reached its apotheosis with Beck's breakout hit "Loser," which launched his very successful Xer-ish career. From Beck's genre-bending music to absurdly sublime lyrics, he mixed and matched nonsense in such a way that his music made perfect sense to a generation increasingly comfortable with ambiguity (be it professional, sexual,

---

**The Baffler*, a very sporadically published journal of cultural criticism, was co-founded in Chicago by Thomas Frank, author of *What's the Matter with Kansas?* But due to its hardcore leftist politics and a hipper-than-thou arrogance, it has remained largely on the fringes, despite having launched several careers. (Thomas Frank and Matt Weiland, *Commodify Your Dissent: Salvos from* The Baffler [New York: W. W. Norton & Company, 1997], 16.)

racial, or otherwise). The song "Loser" captured the Xer outsider status of the pre-dot-com era with the lyrics, "I'm a loser baby, so why don't you kill me," before mocking those losers who secretly want to be winners: "I'm a driver, I'm a winner; things are gonna change, I can feel it."

Simultaneously embracing the notion of loser while mocking it became a contrarian version of insouciant hipness, which, of course, was immediately appropriated as an advertising and marketing gimmick. In a *Baffler* essay in which Thomas Frank asked "Alternative to What?," he wrote:

> So it was only a matter of months after the discovery of "Generation X" that the culture industry sighted an all-new youth movement, whose new looks, new rock bands, and menacing new 'tude quickly became commercial shorthand for the rebel excitement associated with everything from Gen X ads and TV shows to the information revolution. Consumers have been treated to what has undoubtedly been the swiftest and most profound shift of imagery to come across their screens since the 1960s.[3]

The decidedly unfashionable losers were suddenly hip, which prompted accusations of "selling out" by the purists.

Except Generation X was having none of it. John Leland, author of *Hip: The History* (and an Xer himself), dissected the art versus commerce, loser versus hipster dichotomy: "The sellout question gets to the very nature of hip. Is . . . hip essentially a loser ethic that can survive anything but winning?"[4] Gen X decided the answer was: fuck no. There was no way Xers were going to renounce whatever success may come from creative pursuits in order to remain unsullied by commerce. So what if the "dominant paradigm" was co-opting alternative culture? Generation X never claimed to be a card-carrying member of the officially sanctioned "underground." It just sort of started out there mostly by necessity.

Just how irrelevant the sellout question had become can be found in the documentary *Dogtown and Z-Boys,* which tells the story of the Zephyr Team, a group of young Venice Beach outcasts in the early 1970s who revolutionized skateboarding by bringing their surfer moves to asphalt. But the kids were ill-prepared to deal with the popularity and subsequent commercialization of their hobby. The subtext of the movie is how the specter of "selling out" tore the Zephyr Team apart, a mistake that skateboarders who came up after them weren't going to make. Tony Hawk, born in 1968 and skating professionally by the age of twelve, is the most successful skater to come up after the Zephyr Team, and his career contributed to the creation of the first X Games in 1995 (and he can still be seen skating in commercials as he pushes forty years old). Despite having parlayed his talent into lucrative endorsements and eventually a product design business, Hawk has experienced wild financial swings as a result of the sport's waxing and waning popularity over the decades. So, for him, the matter of "selling out" wasn't even a question. Swag is nice, but how do you make a living? In other words, you can't sell out if you never bought in to a false dichotomy of art versus commerce.

"If we lay aside the question of authenticity, which is dubious anyway, hip continues to be relevant not despite its contact with commerce but in proportion to it," wrote Leland. "Commercial hip is less a betrayal of the legacy than part of its natural evolution. With its traffic in enlightenment, its coded language, its viral distribution networks and its framing of the immaterial, hip anticipated and helped shape the information economy that we now live in."[5]

Before Moby became a hugely successful DJ and musician with the release in 1999 of the album *Play*, he described himself as an unknown bald-headed musician mixing sounds in his parents' basement—the picture of loser if there ever was one. And contrary to popular notion, *Play* was not an instant hit. It was badly reviewed, if at all. So when asked by Kurt Andersen, host of the radio show *Studio 360*, if it bothered him that the songs from *Play* had become so closely associated with advertising, Moby had this to say: "When you're licensing music to a TV show or advertisement . . . you're doing it because, in my case, I've made music that I selfishly want people to hear, and the music I've made has never gotten a lot of radio support, so if you want people to hear your music, you have to avail yourself of different means."

"Avail yourself of different means" is precisely the sentiment that has fueled an entire generation—from industrious artists to creative entrepreneurs—such as Lucky Joe Shane, an energetic musician living in the East Village with his actress-wife Kelly and a pug named Brutus. In addition to playing gigs in New York, he writes advertising jingles and does voice-overs. He is also in charge of marketing and promotions for a local café that is a haven for creative types in the East Village. And he also plays at corporate events that his brother puts on around the country. "Selling out has nothing to do with commerce versus art. It has to do with integrity," Joe said over a cup of coffee. "When someone hires me to do a voice-over, that's what I'm there for. It's paying my bills so I can have integrity. I'm thirty-four years old. I'm not willing to pile on the bus with three other guys and go touring."

For eight years Joe's main entrepreneurial/creative pursuit was writing, with two partners, the music and lyrics for a Broadway musical. Through readings and work-shopping, they eventually formed a business partnership with inexperienced but wealthy investors to produce the show themselves. In August 2005 *Once Around the Sun* opened. It was about a year in the life of a musician who makes it big, but in the process has to abandon his friends. The music and lyrics were praised by critics, but the story line was dismissed as cliché. In the era of *Entourage*, the tension between becoming a star and selling out your friends seemed like a plot from another era. Joe agrees:

> I regret telling the story that way. The investors didn't respect our creative vision and we didn't protest, we didn't speak up because we were afraid it would all fall apart. Every single thing that the producers wanted changed, what they thought the audience wanted, were the very things that were criticized, and we knew that was going to happen. That's selling out. Next time around, if we get another shot at it, if we're not happy, fuck it, I'll walk away. I'd rather walk away than go through that again. We put eight years into development. I used to be angrier about it, but the more

> evolved I become as a creative person, the more I realize how lucky I am that I had that experience. I wouldn't trade it for anything, even if it wasn't the hit we had hoped for, and even if it was financially draining.

From artists unwilling to starve to MBAs unwilling to be corporate tools, economic instability inadvertently created an entire generation of practical risk-takers like Joe. Again, and as Hacker points out in *The Great Risk Shift*, during the 1990s educated workers experienced a larger increase in economic volatility than people who did not finish high school. "Prudent choices can reduce but not eliminate exposure to the growing level of economic risk," writes Hacker, a professor of political science at Yale University. "People who are risk-seeking experience wild income swings, but so too do people who are highly risk-averse—which is not at all what one would expect if income volatility were mostly voluntary."[6]

From the moment Xers began entering the workforce, they were changing the workforce. According to statistics from the Small Business Administration released in April 1996, 20 percent of all small-business owners at that time were between the ages of twenty-five and thirty-four. According to another study conducted in 1995, 10 percent of Americans between twenty-five and thirty-four had started a business, which was nearly three times the rate of any other age group.[7] Some back-of-the-envelope calculations in a 1997 *Fast Company* article titled "Free Agent Nation" indicated that 16 percent of the American workforce, or roughly 25 million people, are free agents in the United States, a term this article describes as "people who move from project to project and who work on their own, sometimes for months, sometimes for days." Furthermore, the article argues that the numbers have only grown as Generation X has moved into their prime earning years, thereby defying expectations that once Xers began to age, they would become more prudent and risk-averse.[8]

For those Xers unwilling to role the dice, there was still considerable chafing at the constraints of corporate careerism. This observation was the theme of a largely unread but cleverly written and designed book titled *Day Job: A Workplace Reader for the Restless Age*, by Jonathan Baird, published in 1998. The novel is a spoof within a spoof of the then-current faddish management tool called TQM, or Total Quality Management. This system was adopted from techniques developed in Japan, and it reached its peak in the States in the mid-1990s.*

The protagonist, Mark Thornton, is a customer service drone a few years out of college. One of his clients suggests he keep a self-discovery diary as a way to figure out what he wants to do with his life. At first he dismisses this suggestion as New Age mumbo jumbo, but then has the idea to sell it to his bosses as a "proactive" TQM exercise, which he then uses as both a diversion from his mind-numbing workday and a way to cleverly savage the idiocy of corporate culture by

*According to the International Organization for Standards, "Total quality management is defined as a management approach that tries to achieve and sustain long-term organizational success by encouraging employee feedback and participation, satisfying customer needs and expectations, respecting societal values and beliefs, and obeying governmental statutes and regulations." (http://en.wikipedia.org/wiki/Quality_management.)

mocking TQM language. In the course of keeping this "self-discovery" diary, the protagonist realizes he doesn't have to be stuck in customer service after all: he can utilize his "hobby" as a photographer and designer *within* the company! He will soon be able to transfer out of customer service to the "creative department"—except there's a catch: management fails to detect the sarcasm that's dripping from his TQM journal. Consequently, because he did such a good job in his own diary conveying how helpful TQM can be, he's called back down to teach incoming customer service reps how to keep their own workplace "self-discovery" diaries.

The penultimate irony (because there never seems to be a "final" irony for this generation) might be this: the real-life author and publisher of *Day Job* decided to sell the book only through college and independent bookstores (as well as the Internet, which in 1998 had a mere fraction of the "long-tail" reach it does today). Consequently, the book didn't sell very well. The author might have learned a lesson from the fictional character he created who realized you can never really escape unsullied from commerce, even if you transfer to the creative department. As Leland put it in *Hip: The History*, "That coy pose of selling-out-but-not-really-selling-out is a way to claim a little leverage on a system that in reality allows nothing outside it."[9]

5

WhatGoesUp.com

(Jen Bekman, from hotel switchboard operator to high-flying Internet executive to art gallery owner, as told to the author.)

I grew up a middle-class kid in New York, went to Stuyvesant High School. After college I worked in the hotel business. It was always assumed by me and my parents that I would have a career. So I started out as a switchboard operator at an Ian Schrager hotel. It was like shift work. I went out and listened to jazz every night. I didn't know what I wanted to do. Then I started working in the executive office for the general manager of the Royalton on 44th Street. I was working for this woman, doing special events, press release stuff. She left the hotel to start a company with her husband and asked me to work with her on a new technology venture.

My parents were so mad at me. I was about to be offered a position to do corporate sales at the hotel. They were so happy that I was going to have this career path with benefits. But I was like, "Yeah, no, I'm going to go work with this woman doing stuff." This was before the web had even been invented. We were developing a Bulletin Board System. You could get rich media by dialing up and connecting to a central server. It was used by tech people or for porn—games or porn, basically. So we were developing a BBS that would be updated monthly and it was supposed to be an integrated online arts and entertainment CD-ROM magazine, which was a very different use of the whole BBS medium. The web was invented while I was working there. I remember United Feature Syndicate was posting a *Dilbert* cartoon every day and it was *free!* We were like, this is so *cool!* Anyway, our BBS project failed, shockingly. Ultimately, I think I was fired. Which was fine because I collected unemployment.

I went to work for Omar Wasow at New York Online. Omar and I had gone to Stuyvesant together. He was a huge pioneer in the field and became Oprah's Internet teacher. At the time, he was running a BBS that was used by a lot of people of color, which was very unusual at the time. So I worked for free and collected unemployment from the old job. We started doing website development. It was so fun and interesting and it was all about communications. I loved e-mail and message boards and conferencing. At New York Online, I got to know people who had completely different lives than I did. I just learned so much. It was an exciting time. Omar had a T3 line put into his brownstone in Brooklyn. We were doing stuff that was the new thing. I've always been interested in media, and this was the new media. I saw it as an opportunity to enter a new arena not as an intern or production assistant. At that point, I was in my early twenties.

I worked with Omar until I moved to San Francisco in 1996. I went to visit and decided to move there. I thought, "This is where stuff is really happening." Plus, I had never really lived anywhere but New York. So I bought a one-way ticket and moved out there with a big duffel bag and no job. I ended up getting hired at Electric Minds. It was started by Howard Rheingold, this Marin County kind of guy who had gotten money to do this web-based community project. He had written the book *The Virtual Community*, which came out of his experiences at The WELL, a BBS that had been around since the 1980s. So my first job was director of community for Electric Minds. It was funny on many levels. I got drop-kicked into this Deadhead-Marin-hippy world. Everybody was like, "Don't forget to breathe," and I'm like, "What the fuck are you talking about? We're launching tomorrow and we don't have a plan for tech support escalation!" It was fun. But they didn't get their second round of financing because they didn't come up with a business plan. Everyone talks about the bubble bursting in 2000, but there was a minicontraction in 1997.

After that I consulted for a while. I was considered an authority of online community development, and one of my clients was Netscape, which turned into a full-time job. But Netscape wasn't interested in editorial, so all my efforts in that direction had to be put into some "utility" function, so I left to go to Infoseek, which was being acquired by Disney. So I ended up the director of interactive programming at Disney. I worked there for eighteen months, and all I did was pitch, hold strategy sessions, and make presentations, just trying to convince them to do something. Part of the problem was that I was really young: I was not a seasoned corporate executive. I really didn't know how to conduct myself in that kind of an organization, and it's a very middle-aged male company. On the one hand, I felt important, flying to LA having high-level meetings with Eisner's business development team, but then being completely frustrated because I was totally ineffective.

On a whim, I responded to a job listing in the *Silicon Valley Newsletter* in early 2000 for a consumer-oriented streaming video site, much like YouTube, only this was way before there was enough broadband penetration to make it workable. I responded to this ad not knowing that the job was in New York. So they offered me the job and I kept saying no, I didn't want to move. But they were really persistent. The recruiter flew me out to New York, took me out to dinner. I threw out what I thought was a ridiculous salary. They slapped another $30,000 on top of that, and I just figured it was too much to turn down. They moved me back to New York. I didn't know then that six months later the whole thing was going to implode. I feel like I caught the last train out of San Francisco. I moved back [to New York] in May 2000, and the market had already peaked in March.

I hired a bunch of people over the summer and into the fall, and I noticed that I was getting a lot of job queries—desperate job queries. I felt bad for them, and one day I thought, where would I work if I didn't work here? And I looked at the jobs available and I realized there weren't any jobs for me, either. I knew there was a bubble and it would burst, but I had a lot of experience, so I thought I would work at a big media company. But there were no jobs at big media companies, either. It sucked. When my company went out of business, they owed me a lot of money. I had people who moved here that I had to fire. It was brutal.

I was exhausted and burned-out. Having been caught up in the frenzy for so long, I just had a skewed idea of what mattered. I was out of work for a year and a half. I had some money, but I mostly lived off credit cards and a couple freelance jobs. It just all came apart so quickly. There was too much money being thrown at something that wasn't developed yet. And then the backlash was so severe.

Before the company went under, I was looking at apartments. I was about to move out of my rent-stabilized place in the East Village; I had already put a deposit down on this really expensive place. One night I had this moment of clarity where I sat down and figured out the difference in rent for one year, which was close to $50,000, so I decided to just spend that money renovating the place I was in. Thank god. The renovations were already under way when I lost my job, and I remember the electrician was making fun of me for being an Internet executive. The implication was that I had no skills.

After everything crashed, no one was going to hire me to make web pages. I was always the person who strategized. And that was even less of a marketable skill. Things just became very vocational. What could you produce? What is the thing that you can do? And I couldn't produce anything. A lot of people went back to school.

I had gone to Hunter College, but never graduated. So I tried going back to school, too. I took two classes at Hunter: a modern poetry class and a media studies course. I was getting a lot out of both classes; the professors were great. But I remember there were materials on reserve at the library, and you had to go check out a book and Xerox the material. You had to get a Xerox card and stand in line to photocopy the book. I just had this moment where I was like, "What the fuck?" There was no way I could do it. It just seemed ridiculous. There might be some arrogance in that, but Xeroxing a book seemed completely disconnected from my desire to learn. It wasn't just Xeroxing a book, but everything that represented. After years of working in this new, exciting arena, doing things no one had done before, making money, to then be standing there in line to Xerox a book—needless to say, I didn't finish the classes.

After a year and a half being unemployed, I got a job finally as VP of community at MeetUp.com. On paper it was the perfect job from day one, but it was not the right environment for me. My salary was less than a quarter of what my previous salary had been. But that wasn't even the issue. It was actually really hard because all that time I wasn't working, I thought it was because I didn't want to do anything else but the Internet—that's where my identity was. I had floated around after college not knowing what I wanted to do, so when the Internet started percolating, I thought, "No wonder! The thing I wanted to do didn't exist yet." So I didn't see how I could do anything else. I wasn't going back to the hotel business or getting a law degree. I feel like I can do almost anything; I can be competent at a lot of different things. But my Achilles heel is a sense of entitlement that I want to do something that I enjoy. For me it's always been that way.

Coming to the realization that I was so unhappy in this environment was a shock. I hated it and they knew I hated it. So the MeetUp job ended in September 2002, and I'm out of work again, looking at my finances, and I thought I could cash out my 401k—it was $25,000—and spend it in teaspoons or lay it on the table. So I went looking for an opportunity. I thought about opening a café. But the gallery idea snowballed really quickly.

The idea came about because I was talking to a friend about how to market her photography. Because I had all this experience with building online community, it was a natural transition to do marketing. So we were going to do a show in my apartment, then I was going to rent a place for a month, and then it just escalated. I thought, "Well, if I can find a space to rent in this one particular area and if it has a security gate . . ." So I went for a walk near my apartment and I see this space for rent in exactly the area I wanted to be and it had been a jewelry store, so it had a security gate and closed circuit system. It just seemed like the road came up to meet me at every stage. I had gotten enough signs that this could work, and once that sets in there's no turning back. The gallery opened in March 2003.

The role of the gallery is to support emerging artists and collectors. The philosophy behind the gallery comes from my own experience. I made a lot of money at one time, and I didn't buy any art and no one tried to sell me any. What are the things I've spent money on that are of lasting value? I bought some furniture, which is nice so I don't have to live like a college student. But other than that, I don't know what

I spent my money on. I know there are people out there with disposable income who want to spend it on something with lasting value but feel intimidated by the art world—they feel it's impenetrable. My gallery and the artists I represent exist for those people.

Entering the art world as an outsider is not easy. It's been a major struggle keeping the gallery open. People with less nerve than me would have long ago packed it in. But one of the things I learned going through the whole dot-com bust is that I'm very careful to remember how fortunate I am. A good day, what constitutes a good life, is very elemental. I have a roof over my head and legs that I walk around on and people who love me, and that's pretty good. I'm very privileged, and I know that. The fact that I'm a smart woman, healthy emotionally and physically—my worst day is exponentially better than the vast majority's best day. And that's always been true. I try to stay grounded in that.

That's not to say I don't get caught up in ridiculous things and feel grouchy that I can't have expensive stuff. I'm tired. I have no security. I think that being an entrepreneur . . . it's very lonely. One of the facets of this experience is plumbing the depths of what my tolerance for risk is. It's way higher than I thought it was. I haven't been the most responsible person. The level of chaos and instability in my life often scares people who are close to me.

But I'm living a good life, even if it's different from what I thought it would be. I'm not old enough yet to regret anything. Have this conversation with me when I'm fifty, and it might be different if I'm single and no kids and no savings and no health insurance. I hope that when I'm fifty, I have accomplishments. I hope that I'm never without goals.

One of the constructive things for me is being forced to understand my own criteria for success. It's not contingent on how much money I have in the bank. Just looking at the big picture versus day to day. Do I want to be a big success? Yes. Day to day, am I wasting my time and letting stuff pass me by? No. Am I alive? Yes. I can never be on autopilot. I really feel like I'm challenging myself to do interesting things. I love that I'm not living a life that everyone else is living. I love having the ability to have a positive impact on so many people's lives. I like having my own thing, that it's mine.

6

Funny Weird or Funny Ha-Ha? . . . Hey, Why Limit Yourself!

It's still hard to believe Prince wrote the lyrics "Tonight we're going to party like it's 1999" in 1983. The song may have been about nuclear Armageddon, but still, the fact that in 1999 everyone *was* partying like there was no tomorrow—and not too long into 2000, the party was definitely over—is still rather mind-boggling. The last line of "1999," spoken by a little girl, "Mom, why does everyone have a bomb?" could be substituted with "Mom, why does everyone have a dot-com?"

To get a sense of the prevailing sentiment at the onset of the new millennium and understand how we got there, the best place to turn is Suck.com. The pioneering humor website, created in the early days of the World Wide Web, was often referred to as the online version of *Spy* and/or *Mad* magazine. One of the most popular columns, "Filler," written by Heather Havrilesky (under the name Polly Ester) and illustrated by Terry Colon, rang in the new millennium with its usual good

© Terry Colon, illustrator. Used with permission.

© Terry Colon, illustrator. Used with permission.

© Terry Colon, illustrator. Used with permission.

cheer: "IT'S THE YEAR 2000! And you're still totally irrelevant! Can you believe it?"

This influential website came in the form of snarky humor with a hidden mission to change how the vanguard of the Internet revolution was running things. But readers weren't getting hit over the head with the intent of the website; they didn't know the intent *at all*. Loyal eyeballs just returned to Suck day after day to partake of the inside joke. As the creators dubbed a collection of the best posts, "Worst-Case Scenarios in Media, Culture, Advertising, and the Internet," Suck was one of the first virtual experiences that fomented a community around humor, turning the old saw "guess you had to be there" on its head. You didn't have to "be there" in a physical sense to get it; you had to be there in an experiential sense, which no longer required actually being there.

The *intent* of the website, however, was to undermine the prevailing wisdom that dominated the early days of the Internet, which at the time was controlled largely by utopian-minded baby-boomers, particularly on the West Coast. Like most "revolutionary" acts perpetrated by Generation X, it was carried out as an inside job with a smart-aleck sense of humor. The first post, on August 28, 1995, set the tone: "At Suck, we abide by the principle which dictates that somebody will always position himself or herself to systematically harvest anything of value in this world for the sake of money, power and/or ego-fulfillment. We aim to be that somebody."

But according to an authoritative retelling of the Suck story by KeepGoing.org, the real purpose of the website, created by Carl Steadman and Joey Anuff, was to show their bosses effective web design.[1] The two worked for *HotWired*, the online publication of *Wired* magazine, which essentially appropriated print elements to the website, such as a title page (or entry page) and an index. This also meant that two or sometimes three click-throughs were required before any content could be accessed.

Suck, on the other hand, had no registration requirements (for easy linkage), and the site's content opened immediately, with simple black type against a white background in a single, narrow column in the center of the page. Even more revolutionary, new content was posted every day at a time when *HotWired* was monthly (monthly!).

One thing that management at *Wired* did get right was encouraging innovation, so employees were allowed to hook up a server to

© Terry Colon, illustrator. Used with permission.

© Terry Colon, illustrator. Used with permission.

© Terry Colon, illustrator. Used with permission.

the company's mainframe and post their own content, which is exactly what the creators of Suck did—except they did it anonymously. So when Suck went live—generating an immediate buzz in the small but influential online world—only one person at *Wired* (other than the creators) knew it was being published from inside the office.

As Matt Sharkey wrote for KeepGoing.org, "Suck spoke to the grunts on the front lines, those like Steadman and Anuff, who saw the mistakes being made at the top but lacked the power to do anything about it. It was snarky and sarcastic. . . . For the ground-level tech drone stuck at a computer, it provided the perfect daily respite. It was quickly located, easily digestible, and if you could suppress your laughter, it looked just like working."[2]

Cracking up the grunts on the front lines, however, was really just a pretext for speaking truth to power: the creators of Suck thought they knew how to do it better than the good old boys running *Wired*, who quickly came to the same realization. Shortly after the debut of Suck, editors scrambled to make *HotWired* daily, and once management found out Suck was coming out of *Wired*'s own office, they bought it. This allowed Anuff and Steadman to work on their own creation full-time during daylight hours and earn a living. Inevitable accusations of "selling out" ensued.

This American Life, a radio program created by Ira Glass, would seemingly have little in common with Suck. But both were launched about the same time, both were motivated by a desire to show how their respective media could be used differently, and both used humor to make their larger point.

PASSAGE TO INSIGNIFICANCE

Choosing Your Own Irrelevant Path

CHOOSE ONE!	
The Irrelevant Slave to a Gaggle of Even Less Relevant Little Pants-Crappers	So you've come to terms with the fact that you'll never amount to shit, that everything you do will end in failure at best or in mediocre insignificance at worst. Good work.
The Very Fashionable Yet Still Completely Irrelevant City Dweller	Now all you have left to do is choose which brand of irrelevance you'd like to achieve. Remember, contrary to the so-called American Dream, not everyone need be an Irrelevant Suburban Family Man (see also: Doo-Doo Wiping Dodo).
The Irrelevant Lover of Good Music Written by Some Much Less Irrelevant Musician	Why, perhaps you'll march to the beat of a different but still totally irrelevant drummer! Procreate and bring into the world yet another thoroughly irrelevant person, or create irrelevant art that no one will ever appreciate—or even see! The possibilities, as always, are limited . . .
The Very Intelligent Lover of Great Books Written By Someone Even More Intelligent and Much, Much More Relevant	
The Irrelevant Creative Type Who Creates Utterly Irrelevant Stuff That Mostly Impresses His Very Irrelevant Mother	
The Very Mellow Person Who's So Comfortable With His Irrelevance that He Devotes Large Blocks of Time to Growing Plants and Other Depressingly Irrelevant Things	
The Irrelevant Overworked Rich Person Who Spends Large Sums of Money on Trying to Feel Less Irrelevant	
The Irrelevant Slacker Who Smokes Multiple Bong Hits and Listens Closely to Old Yes Albums to Achieve an Illusion of Relevance in the World	
The Irrelevant Hollywood Wannabe Who Dreams of Becoming Relevant Every Waking Hour of the Day (See also: Irrelevant Purgatory)	
The Irrelevant Web Writer Whose Only Joy in Life Comes from Humiliating Her Friends in Her Column, or from Creating Imaginary Scenarios in Which Large Canadian Rabbits Beat Aforementioned Friends Within an Inch of Their Lives	

Radio, of course, is a very old medium for storytelling and humor, but not much of either was happening where Glass cut his teeth: National Public Radio.

Glass worked at WBEZ in Chicago for years before developing *This American Life*. Despite his long relationship with NPR, he was unable to convince them to syndicate the show, so he hustled it himself. Even after getting picked up by more than one hundred stations, NPR still declined to get behind the show (Public Radio International finally became its distributor). Perhaps if Glass had been able to create a buzz by anonymously producing the show from inside the offices of Chicago Public Radio, NPR would have courted him the way *Wired* courted Suck. But Glass would do well enough on his own, winning awards and expanding his audience—largely a Gen X demographic. At the time, most media outlets would have fallen over themselves to attract this age group, which Glass did by crafting stories that combined narrative nonfiction with a sardonic sense of humor.* The show would launch entire careers for humorous storytellers, such as David Sedaris, Sarah Vowell, David Raykoff, and others.

While not all of *This American Life* is comedy, it has roots in the alternative comedy world, which got a toehold in the early 1990s, cultivating comedians such as David Cross and Sarah Silverman and Patton Oswalt, best known for doing the voice-over for the rat in *Ratatouille*. As Oswalt told the *New York Times*:

> The model for success as a comedian had always been that you spent your entire career focusing on putting together

*Sardonic, derived from the Greek *sardonios*, is similar to sarcastic, but meant to cause amusement more than insult. The reference comes from eating a Sardinian plant, which was said to produce facial convulsions resembling horrible laughter, usually followed by death!

> one killer five-minute act, you go on "The Tonight Show," get called over to Johnny Carson's desk and get a sitcom. That's how you made it. So I'd started down that path. And then Johnny quit, and that entire model was shattered, which I thought was great. Because instead of performing for an invisible talent scout that wasn't there, we started doing comedy for ourselves, because we just loved doing stand-up. Instead of waiting for this one five-minute shot that decides your whole life, comedy went back to what it was supposed to be: just going onstage and venting and spewing and having fun.[3]

The structural change of comedy came about in part because the comedy club boom of the 1980s had gone bust. Maureen Taran, a manager of comedic talent, told *Spin* magazine: "What happened to comedy in the late 1980s is what happens with everything in America: Make it bigger and it will be better. Instead of controlling the quality, the industry kept pumping out more shows that featured stand-ups, and business people opened comedy clubs as if they were pizza parlors."[4]

Once the pizza parlor–comedy clubs shut down, comedians started performing in rock venues and other alternative spaces, which allowed for experimentation and innovation. Instead of the traditional setup/punch-line style of stand-up, alternative comedy was more about storytelling, intellectual and absurdist humor, improv, and the "comedy of discomfort," later perfected by Sacha Baron Cohen in *Borat*. In the early 1990s, however, the audience for these emerging subgenres of humor was small, and there was even less money in it. But the creative atmosphere changed dramatically, setting the stage for long-term careers—performing, writing, producing, and managing—from Comedy Central to the Internet. How this might come together, however, was not apparent until the dot-com bubble burst.

Erin Keating caught the comedy bug young, and as always for Generation X, it was rooted in the changing landscape of middle-class life. Her parents divorced when she was two, and her mom remained in the Maryland suburbs while her dad moved to downtown Baltimore—an unusual choice for a middle-aged white man in the 1970s. She stated, "Watching *Saturday Night Live* was my reward for custody weekends. It was a no-rules atmosphere. My dad didn't care if I stayed up late and heard inappropriate things. Roseanne Roseannadanna. The killer bees. The land shark. There was a level of absurdity that kids understood."

In high school Erin was involved in school plays and musicals, but the instability of choosing a life of acting dissuaded her initially from pursuing it as a career: "I had gone to prep school and it felt like I was throwing everything away if I went just to an acting school. So I went to NYU for the first two years of college, feeling jealous of everyone in the BFA program. They were all in my dorm, including Sarah Silverman. I was conflicted about taking the safe route. So I took a semester off. I knew I was going back to college, and I was going to be a theater major. I had always wanted to go to Oberlin, so I transferred there and did a lot of experimental theater. I directed. I did my own performance art. My first solo piece was autobiographical; it was all about my defining struggles: my weight and my fractured family. Very self-serious and not very funny.

"Then I moved to San Francisco and was invited to join a sketch comedy group. It was my own version of *SNL*. I had been doing this serious acting training, but I really found myself on this stage. The process was fun. It was smart. It was absurdist. My favorite sketch, I was the wife of a plastic surgeon who experimented on me, so I had tits all over me. I had tits on my back, tits on my knees."

In order to support her comedy habit, Erin worked in the burgeoning San Francisco dot-com world: "I've always worked for entrepreneurs. I respond to that energy, that 'let's put on a show' energy, the DIY ethic. I'm just not an institutional person. My first job was with a consumer technology PR agency. Amazon was a client. Jeff Bezos would be walking around the office and we'd be talking about whether people would actually want to buy books online. I became a business development manager, no really! I did PowerPoint presentations. I knew nothing about technology, but I'm a good writer and that always got me by. There were three of us doing this job. We were in this room and they would run in and be like, 'We're going to RadioShack! Write a pitch!'"

Erin eventually moved to New York to be a "real" actress, but was again drawn to comedy and supported herself through Internet work: "I had one last good contact in the dot-com world, so I got a job with a consumer data company that supplied info to catalogues. I knew it was the end when I went to a sales conference in Little Rock, Arkansas, when a twentysomething-year-old said, 'I love being part of the old boys' network.' I was like, 'What the fuck? What am I doing here?'

"It wasn't until the dot-com thing started to die that I began producing shows off Broadway and learned how to be a development person. It was a serious hit in terms of money, but I realized there were jobs in this business that weren't acting. A producer is paid to put a team together and make it happen."

After a stint at Comedy Central, Erin eventually landed an opportunity that combined both comedy and the Internet: she is now a producer for one of the many proliferating humor websites. Although Web 2.0 has been far less speculative, it's still a highly uncertain job, and yet she's grateful to have it because she can earn a living and also cultivate creativity, so long as it lasts: "The job itself is creatively fulfilling, but it's not exactly a secure environment. That's what I chose. And in some ways, it's a relief. Comedy is not always so deep but it's honest. There are the people who are social critics and say the true things that we think but we don't say. But even when it's not about that, comedy doesn't work if it's not true. Beyond my love of just laughter and creativity, it's this sort of willingness to be honest about what life feels like."

The Act of Creation, written in 1964 by Arthur Koestler, is one of the few attempts to include humor in an analysis of the creative process in a systematic way. Koestler, a Hungarian Jew and a public intellectual who once dated Simone de Beauvoir and experimented with LSD,[5] argued that three things—humor, discovery (i.e., science and innovation), and art—are related acts of creation.

> I . . . make a distinction between the routine skills of thinking on a single "plane," as it were, and the creative act, which, as I shall try to show, always operates on more than

> one plane. The former may be called single-minded, the latter a double-minded, transitory state of unstable equilibrium where the balance of both emotion and thought is disturbed. . . . The result (as I hope to show) is either a *collision* ending in laughter, or their *fusion* in a new intellectual synthesis, or their *confrontation* in an aesthetic experience.

To illustrate the point, he uses the image of a rounded triptych representing three domains of creativity that shade into each other without sharp boundaries: "The first is intended to make us laugh; the second to make us understand; the third to make us marvel. The logical pattern is the same in all three cases; it consists in the *discovery of hidden similarities*. . . . The common denominator of these heterogeneous emotions is a feeling of participation, identification, or belonging; in other words, the self is experienced as being a *part of a larger whole*."[6]

Modern social scientists of the *Bowling Alone** ilk have lamented the fragmentation—if not complete breakdown—of community. And yes, traditional modes of connecting with a larger community have declined, i.e., bowling leagues, church groups, extended familial relationships, etc. But that isn't the

*In *Bowling Alone: The Collapse and Revival of American Community*, Robert D. Putnam exhaustively documents the collapse but not the revival of community. He concludes his analysis with a set of possible "solutions," which sound ridiculous to the Gen X ear, such as educational programs, work-based initiatives, and funded community service programs, to bring people back together. This would be about as appealing and effective as abstinence-only sex education for teens or classes about the importance of marriage for single mothers. What's more, it misses the creative culture and economy that have grown up as a result. (New York: Simon & Schuster, 2001.)

whole story. It is no wonder that the most creative acts—humor, innovation, and art, which bring about that sense of being part of a larger whole—are flourishing at the same time that traditional community has broken down, which tended to dampen individuality and creativity through social controls. It is in this milieu that a generation came of age, creating a kind of econo-socio-cultural feedback loop. As the economy fragmented, so did traditional community, thereby allowing creativity to flow (however painful that may be), which created new ways of connecting and forming community.

Of course, the old order doesn't go down without a fight—and in fact never really disappears completely—especially when money is involved. What started out as a small utopian community that believed technology could change the world became a milieu for innovation and discovery, which ultimately became tragic as the financial bubble ensued—a modern-day tulip frenzy of unprecedented proportions. The bubble sucked up resources and creativity, which ultimately became corrupted by the absurd amount of venture capital being thrown around.

Despite the creative energy rushing into Web. 1.0, much like the 1980s comedy club boom writ large, the American way is to take something successful and make it bigger until it collapses in on itself. It's not so much that bigger is bad, but rather that the central purpose is much more easily lost as the quest changes from creation to self-perpetuation. Then, once the original vision is gone, it's a slippery slope to irrational exuberance.

As pointed out by Roger Lowenstein, author of *Origins of the Crash,* a small online retailer, eToys, was worth three times as much as Toys R Us, even though eToys had revenue of $25 million while the revenue stream of Toys R Us was $11 billion. It's not much of a leap from that to Enron, Worldcom, and Tyco International CEO Dennis Kozlowski with his $6,000 shower curtain and a $2 million birthday party for his wife. (He is currently serving up to twenty-five years for grand larceny, conspiracy, and securities fraud.)

Of course, some people did quite well during the boom. For the typical Gen Xer, however, the opportunity costs of embarking on a risky gold rush were compounded by getting financially burned in the stock market crash. In fact, Generation X had more of its total assets invested in the stock market during the bubble years than any other age group.[7]

What's more, the post-bubble recession was yet another whammy for Xers. Usually recessions hit the youngest workers the hardest, which was certainly true in the early 1990s when Xers were the youngest workers. But in the post-bubble recession, midcareer workers were hit just as hard as the youngest workers, which is a particularly devastating blow at a time when getting professional traction is critical.[8]

In past recessions, job loss was as much cyclical as it was structural (i.e., you got rehired when things picked up, as opposed to having to find a job in an entirely new sector, usually for less pay). But according to a 2003 report for the Federal Reserve Bank of New York, much of the post-bubble job loss was structural, setting the stage for a "jobless" recovery. The authors wrote:

> The downturns in the mid-1970s and early 1980s show an even mix of cyclical and structural adjustments. That is,

> during these episodes, about half of employment was in industries affected structurally and half in industries affected cyclically. The pattern changed in the early 1990s, when industries undergoing structural adjustments increased their share of total employment to 57 percent. The greatest change, however, is apparent in the 2001 downturn, when 79 percent of employees worked in industries affected more by structural shifts than by cyclical shifts.[9]

So what to do? Make some jokes about the absurdity of life. After all, history repeats itself first as tragedy, then as farce. *Avenue Q*, one of the biggest Broadway musical hits in years (which won the Tony in 2004), is a takeoff of *Sesame Street* that gives gallows-humor treatment to topics near and dear to the Gen X heart: unaffordable housing (more on this in Chapter 11), cyclical joblessness, and the search for "purpose" in one's life. The main character, Princeton, is unemployed, in debt, and alone. But not to worry: things might suck at the moment, but hey, "Everything in life is only for now," the characters sing insouciantly.

Even the aftermath of 9/11 was put in an incongruous context by David Rees, creator of the comic *Get Your War On*, in which clip-art office characters say ridiculous things to each other about war and terrorism. It immediately became one of those Internet sensations and, within a matter of months, Rees had a deal with *Rolling Stone* magazine. At a talk Rees gave at Columbia University, a student asked about his motivation to create the strip. His first answer was a joke, of course: "I wasn't sure I was up for a never-ending battle between good and

Get Your War On, © 2001 by David Rees. Used with permission

evil—it seemed really expensive and exhausting." But then he began expounding on a very Gen X attitude about the role of popular culture in America: "I have this really romantic notion of American pop culture, this idea that you can have popular expression that is really accessible, that is not using elitist language . . . and that pop culture can present itself as an entertaining counter-argument to whatever gigantic narrative that is being laid down on the population by the powers that be."[10]

It is no wonder then that comedy and humor proliferated in the aftermath of the dot-com bubble absurdity. As Koestler explains in *The Act of Creation*, laughter is a "luxury reflex." It "rings the bell of man's departure from the rails of instinct; it signals his rebellion against the singlemindedness of his biological urges, his refusal to remain a creature of habit, governed by a single set of 'rules of the game'." This luxury reflex known as laughter could arise only in an evolved creature that can realize, "I have been fooled."[11]

7

Gonna Get Me Some Happy

The concept of happiness has been kicked around for eons by everyone from Buddha to Oprah. But for one independent filmmaker, *Happiness* is a movie that is about as dark a comedy as a director can get away with in America (and the director, Todd Solondz, almost didn't get away with it). Various forms of sexual dysfunction and exploitation are explored through this ensemble cast of desperate, despicable, self-absorbed characters who are as alienated from themselves as they are from each other. The comedy comes about, in part, by scoring these twisted scenes like an "After School Special," creating hilarious juxtapositions between sight and sound. And then there is a kind of extreme Seinfeldian treatment, in which these solipsistic personalities deal with the dark side of life ever so blithely. One character, played by Lara Flynn Boyle, is a bestselling author who has written about childhood rape. In a moment of existential crisis, she soliloquizes, "Everything I write is shallow! Can't anyone see through me? . . . If only I'd been raped as a child. Then I'd know authenticity."

In a little Gen X lovefest, writer Jonathan Lethem (just before publishing his acclaimed novel *Motherless Brooklyn*) reviewed *Happiness* for *Salon*, saying it "might" be a masterpiece. One reason he didn't make a more sure-footed statement was the brouhaha that surrounded the film at the time. One of the plotlines involves a child molester, so cue up the controversy: people complained that a comedy, no matter how dark, shouldn't treat such despicable acts with anything less than moral outrage and horror (which of course it does in its own twisted way). This caused Universal Studios, the corporate distributor of Solondz's first and well-received film *Welcome to the Dollhouse*, to drop *Happiness*, even after it won an International Critic's Prize for Best Film at the Cannes film festival.

In order to get the movie out, the highly acclaimed independent production company that funded the movie, Good Machine, formed its own distribution arm and released it independently in 1998. A founding principal of Good Machine, James Schamus, made a presentation at an arts and culture conference at the University of Chicago titled "The Pursuit of Happiness: Making an Art of Marketing an Explosive Film." He said that getting the film distributed was only one in a series of challenges. Getting the film funded in the first place also took some creativity.

Schamus explained: "Rather than sell the film's stories and characters, we sold its 'philosophy.' The film, we said, was about the crisis of overproduction in America today. 'Overproduction?' the perplexed film executive would ask. 'Yes, the overproduction of desire,' we would explain. 'You see, each year America spends about one-third of its Gross National Product on advertising and marketing, in a frantic attempt to create and sustain enough desire in people that they'll want to buy all the crap we and the Chinese and everyone else is producing so that we can continue to despoil the environment and hasten our demise through global warming. . . . The average American has too much desire to know what to do with, and it is in the disposition of this excess desire, in the inability of the social structure to absorb it properly, that trouble starts in suburbia. And that's what *Happiness* is about.'"[1]

Whew! Now that's a tough sell. It's surprising the film got funded at all, and it's no wonder that the corporate distributor, Universal, owned by a publicly traded company (Seagrams), dropped it once the dust storm got kicked up. But rather than rail against "The Man" for quashing their creative freedom, which would do nothing but back everyone into a corner, the innovative thinkers at Good Machine saw it as an opportunity, as Schamus went on to explain:

> Clearly, they didn't want the film to be sold to another distributor, and we didn't want it retained by Universal. But Good Machine could distribute it. And if Universal wanted to be seen as morally good and true, it would have to cut a deal with us that would enable us to support the film's release appropriately. I can't speak to the confidential financing and banking agreements that allowed for all this, but at

> the end of the day, we had a film that benefited in the marketplace by being both suppressed and promoted by one and the same system.

So it would seem that one definition of happiness for Gen X is the ability to translate creative freedom into market share. Or, to put it another way, turn bitter lemons into lemonade.

From Aristotle to the framers of the U.S. Constitution, happiness has historically been thought of as a pursuit rooted in action, not a state of mind or being. But the baby-boomers decided they didn't like that, and so they developed a concept of happiness based on the philosophy that you can think your way into it: no action required. Just step away from the Freudian analysis of pathology, and you're well on your way to bliss—or at least moving away from misery. This philosophy, which is behind the recent proliferation of most happiness studies, books, college courses, Oprah shows, and conferences, is rooted in the positive psychology movement and traceable to baby-boomer self-indulgence. Ellen Langer, a professor of psychology at Harvard, told *New York* magazine that the positive psychology theory of happiness, "like so many cultural curiosities involving self-obsession, [is] a boomer phenomenon."[2]

But there is a parallel happiness studies trend currently under way that is instead rooted in economics. Until very recently, economists measured happiness purely from an outcome perspective. That is, whatever choices people made were based on rational desires. Thus, wealth must make people happy since they pursue it so vigorously. There was no attempt to measure if in fact wealth made people happy because that is not really measurable using traditional economic tools. The more recent approach to the economics of happiness, however, does not assume that outcomes are necessarily the result of rational decision making. While taking psychology into consideration, a new approach to the economics of happiness tries to determine what exactly makes people happy and to make recommendations based on circumstances that people can actually change.

Not only do these studies show happiness is not so much about innate personality or positive thinking (as the psychologists argue), but one's level of happiness is partly the result of choices and actions. But these choices and actions aren't necessarily rational. Because people pursue outcomes all the time that lead to considerable unhappiness, it's important to figure out what in fact does contribute to well-being. As Harvard professor of psychology Daniel Gilbert has documented in his book, *Stumbling on Happiness*, that people are incredibly bad at predicting what will make them happier (although he is firmly rooted in the positive psychology, set-point theory of happiness).

In *Building a Better Theory of Well-Being*, Richard A. Easterlin, a professor of economics at the University of Southern California, argues that over the course of one's life, changes in circumstances with regard to family, health, and work do have a lasting impact on one's happiness. This contradicts the "set-point" theory in which innate personality determines one's level of happiness with little variation—even after tragic happenstance or great good fortune. An example often used by the set-point proponents is the person who has had a debilitating accident that resulted in permanent disability, but six months later is about as happy as she was before the accident. Easterlin argues that over the course of one's life, people with disabilities are considerably less happy than people without, and that this long-term analysis is a much more accurate way of measuring happiness.

Easterlin's studies show—and others confirm—that the one consistent category in which better circumstances do not increase happiness over one's lifetime is financial wealth.[3] Above a certain threshold (a rather low one at that), increased wealth has little to do with higher reported rates of well-being. Whereas better health and increasing satisfaction with family life do create more happiness, satisfaction about increased wealth is short-lived, and the pursuit for more of it goes on endlessly. This is often referred to as the "hedonic treadmill," resulting in "the overproduction of desire," as Schamus, the producer of *Happiness*, put it. Easterlin also argues that because material/financial gains don't make people happier, people should spend more time with their families and improving their health—both of which influence people's long-term level of happiness—and less time pursuing work.

But here is where Easterlin misses a critical point for Generation X. His studies show that improved circumstances around work also have a positive effect on one's well-being, but because he associates work with the pursuit of wealth, he recommends reducing work in order to spend more time improving health and family life. (He also has nothing to say about social life or friendship, which is another huge oversight, particularly for Generation X. More on that in Chapter 8.) To assume that work is only about making money is an old-fashioned notion. If work is an intellectual or creative pursuit—which it is more for Xers than for previous generations—and has less to do with material gain, then spending less time working would not increase happiness.

Easterlin's analysis also shows that people do not seem to learn that having more money is not making them happier, and that this "misperception has major societal consequences, because [it] condemns us to the pursuit of unending economic growth."[4] But that too might be changing with Generation X, which has consistently reported that balance in one's life is more important than amassing more wealth and climbing the corporate ladder—even if that means living with less. Surveys consistently show that Gen Xers say it's important to them that work is personally fulfilling as much as financially rewarding. Indeed, Gen Xers are often willing to give up some financial gains for more fulfilling work.[5] Gen X women in particular seem well suited to the changing landscape of work and the pursuit of happiness, according to a 1998 article in *The Independent* (London):

> Feminism has made a great impact on Generation Xers . . . with women generally having a more positive outlook, being more prepared to take risks and adapt to change. "Generation X women are self-confident, fairly empowered and are not necessarily trying on all these different guises," said Jane Falkingham, lecturer on population studies and social policy at the London School of Economics.[6]

MaryAnn Johansen, born in 1969, identifies herself as both a feminist and a Gen Xer, and hates that both terms are often derided. "I never much thought about it, but, like 'feminist,' when 'Generation X' started to become a negative term is about when I started identifying with it." Of course, the stereotype of a feminist Xer screams 'humorless miserable human being,' and by any traditional measure, MaryAnn should be unhappy. Neither married nor financially secure, she doesn't own her own home nor does she have kids; she has no health insurance or even a car. And she works all the time. Yet she describes herself as reasonably happy, and not the least bit interested in collecting the things that most people think of as the talismans of happiness. Why? Because she enjoys her work as a writer, which she finds creatively fulfilling, and, as a freelancer, she is in control of her time. This is a sentiment echoed repeatedly by Xers who, once freed from the nine-to-five life, are willing to endure substantial risk in order to avoid ever having to go back to it.

"I was on staff at various magazines from '88 to '95 when I quit because I couldn't stand the corporate bullshit anymore. I was at the Book of the Month Club at the time. I came to a realization: no matter how efficiently you worked and no matter how good of a job you did, it was all about looking like you were totally devoted to the company. If you worked hard and left at 6:00, you were not seen as a good employee. If you futzed around and stayed till 8:00, you were a team player. It's completely asinine. So I had some money saved up, and I didn't know what I was going to do, but I quit. And immediately people asked me to freelance, so that was confirmation I did the right thing."

That wasn't the first time MaryAnn looked around at her life, realized she was not on the right course, and took action to change her circumstances (a key ingredient for happiness). Growing up on Long Island, MaryAnn developed a love of film and decided to go to NYU film school, but dropped out after two years: "It was not at all how I thought it was going to be. I had this romantic idea of how I was going to do guerilla filmmaking on the streets of New York City. But it was like going through a film school mill where they drive any kind of creativity out of you. And it was extremely expensive. My parents were not wealthy by any stretch of the imagination, so I felt guilty about that. So it just didn't seem worth it. While I was in film school, I wrote and published science fiction fanzines; I'm a real geek. So I got my first job in publishing because of my 'zines."

In addition to freelance writing and editing, MaryAnn fulfills her love of film through her website, Flick Filosopher, which she started in 1997, as well as writing reviews for other publications: "The focus of my life has been my work. That might sound kind of sad, but it's what's made me happy. But I haven't had health insurance for years. And the economy after 9/11 was really bad. So I have a huge amount of debt from that. I've been spending the last couple of years paying down this debt. At one point I thought I was going to have to get a real job, and that just puts this horrible dread in me, thinking what those places do to people, putting them through such a grind, working sixty hours a week, and for what? A magazine? So luckily, now I'm at the point that I'm making money."

MaryAnn is able to piece together enough to live comfortably in Woodlawn, the northernmost point of the Bronx, but she doesn't expect to be able to own a house. "Which is fine with me, because I don't want that. This whole American Dream thing, that's so not me. It would be nice to have more money, but I wouldn't spend it on a house. I would travel and do less work. The idea of being a slave to a mortgage is not appealing. Part of it is having lived in the suburbs as a kid. We lived in the Bronx until I was seven and then moved way out on Long Island so my parents could afford to buy a house. My father has been doing this long commute, two and a half hours, for years.

"I'm just not pining away for the house, the marriage, and kids. People say they want these things, but it's always in a nebulous way. I can imagine wanting to be married to a specific person, but just wanting to be married in an abstract sense? I don't get that. I don't feel strongly about having kids or not. If I have kids it would be with someone in particular who I wanted to have kids with. I'm alone but not lonely. And I have lots of close friends and an active social life. I could meet someone tomorrow and fall in love and everything could change. But being with someone for the sake of it is another kind of hell. A lot of people don't understand not wanting to have the security of a job and a relationship. I'm probably too independent for my own good."

Happiness studies, including Easterlin's, consistently show that people in long-term relationships are happier than single people (and there is no difference between married couples and people who cohabitate).[7] So in that respect, MaryAnn might be somewhat unusual. But what seems consistent among many of the happiness studies is that people feel better when they are in control of their own time and lives—as MaryAnn is—and have the ability to adapt to changing circumstances and adjust expectations. Indeed, surveys and studies consistently show that expectations about wealth play an enormous role in whether or not people say they are happy. And this explains a great deal of Generation X's attitude about money and the pursuit of happiness.

Ironically, before this generation was known as Generation X, the prevailing wisdom (circa 1985) was that this group would have it pretty cushy in almost every way: as baby-boomers aged their way through society, vast opportunities would open up for the smaller demographic coming up behind them; colleges would be *competing* with each other to attract the best students; as boomers moved out of the workforce there would be more jobs available than could be filled, increasing pay, and benefits; and—get this—there would be a flood of affordable housing as boomers traded up![8] As the saying goes, prediction is very hard, especially about the future.

From having been set up for disappointment, an interesting contradiction emerges. According to research conducted by the Pew Research Center for the People and the Press, compared with other demographic groups, Gen X ranks itself lower on the ladder of life in terms of economic well-being,[9] and yet report greater happiness compared to demographic groups immediately younger and older.[10] This seeming contradiction is in fact consistent with the recent spate of studies about the economics of happiness. Generation X, having been whipsawed by the economy, has come to expect less material wealth: 34 percent of Gen Xers assume they will have to work beyond retirement age, compared to only 22 percent of those eighteen to twenty-nine and 30 percent of people fifty and older.[11] These lowered expectations have freed people to pursue the things that actually make a difference in one's sense of well-being. Indeed, another key ingredient to an overall level of happiness is not to expect to be happy all the time.

Where did the expectation come from that people should, by default, feel "happy" anyway? Generation X, always a little disdainful of New Age bullshit, has kind of relished its unhappiness, as embodied in characters such as Ethan Hawke's Troy Dyer in *Reality Bites*, the 1994 film about post-college Gen X angst. Dyer is a serially unemployed philosopher-musician who touches on the existential crisis experienced by Xers, which initially seems to be depressing and cynical, but could very well be the secret to this generation figuring out what really makes people happy: "There's no point to any of this. It's all just a . . . a random lottery of meaningless tragedy and a series of near escapes. So I take pleasure in the details. You know . . . the sky about ten minutes before it starts to rain, the moment where your laughter becomes a cackle."

Generation X's willingness to embrace unhappiness might be one of the reasons they end up scoring higher on the happy scale in demographic studies. An explanation for this can be found in *The Science of Happiness*, which makes a connection between the physical brain and societal/psychological explanations for happiness. The opposite of happy turns out not to be unhappy, as the way desire and revulsion can be seen as opposite patterns in brain scans. Images of people with happy and unhappy brains don't show similarly opposing patterns: "Only the left half of the cerebellum, for example, is active during happy moments, but when a person is sad, angry or fearful, both sides are working hard."[12] In other words, happy is simple, but unhappy is a bit more complex—and complexity is exactly what Generation X was weaned on.

Generation X has evolved the concept of happiness from "having it all" to achieving balance; from a psychological emphasis to meaningful pursuits—through work or creative expression; from hippy-dippy "inner peace" to a kind of embrace of complexity. This complexity results in the contradiction that, despite seeming somewhat cynical and pessimistic, Generation X reports also being rather happy. What's more, psychologist Alice Isen has determined that being happy facilitates creativity, flexible thinking, and the ability to come up with alternative solutions to solving problems.[13] So Generation X, being realistic and adaptable, may very well be perfectly suited to lead the way into the twenty-first century. Generation X recognizes not only that an "overproduction of desire" is making people miserable, as the movie *Happiness* was critiquing, but also that the hedonic treadmill could very well be hastening the demise of the world as we know it. The first step in dealing with such monumental problems that the world is facing, from economic instability to global warming, is not to expect to be happy all the time, and then to learn how to live *well* with less.

8

Friends: The Newish New Thing

Freelance writer and armchair sociologist Ethan Watters had an epiphany about how friends had become the new family while he and his "tribe" were at Burning Man. This neo-hippy, city-building festival—where a lot of dancing, drugs, performance art, and "sharing" take place, the culmination of which is the burning of a large manlike sculpture on the sixth day—has been held every year since 1990 in Black Rock Desert, a dry lakebed in northwestern Nevada. Having blown off his girlfriend to act like a goof for a week with 25,000 other people in a "manmade" temporary city, he realized that his friends were the most important relationships in his life (as opposed to admitting he just wasn't that into her . . .). Like any enterprising freelance writer, he turned his little aha moment into an article for the *New York Times Sunday* magazine, which got him on TV and inevitably a book contract. Gotta love those trend articles–turned–books.* Or not.

In *Urban Tribes: A Generation Redefines Friendship, Family and Commitment* (which, for unknown reasons, was changed to *Urban Tribes: Are Friends the New Family?* in later versions of the book), Watters tries to make the case that Generation Xers are delaying marriage *because* of such rich friendships. But he got the cause-and-effect relationship exactly backward: nonfamilial relationships have become increasingly important *in part* because people are getting married later in life for reasons that are much more complex (more on that in the next chapter).

Watters's forays into other explanations for why adult friendships have become important to this generation are equally absurd. Urban tribes, he speculates, had developed because Xers had lots of disposable income and plenty of time to spend it with their friends. Maybe for a short period in the late 1990s, particularly in San Francisco where Watters lives, did people have to "duck and cover to stay out of the way of a decent paycheck," but that was an aberration, not the norm. Even when the party was over, according to Watters, money just wasn't an issue. "In the long run, most of us knew we had an ace in the hole. Many of us were in line to be the beneficiaries of the largest transfer of wealth that had ever taken place from one generation to the next." Without citation, Watters goes on: "Something close to $10 trillion . . .

---

*Of course, that is precisely what this book is, which started out as an article for the *New York Observer* titled "Generation X: Born Under a Bad Economic Sign."

was in the process of being passed down to baby boomers *and Generation Xers.*"[1]

Say what? Not only is this inheritance going directly to boomers—not Xers—but the supposedly largest transfer of wealth in the history of humankind is a myth, according to *American Demographics.* In addition to some $8 trillion lost in the post-bubble stock market meltdown, Americans are living longer and need more for retirement, not to mention there are 78 million baby-boomers. "Boomers are too numerous to expect a windfall," economist Laurence Kotlikoff told *American Demographics.* "I'm sorry to burst anyone's bubble, but there's no economic justification for any bonanza inheritance."[2]

Making matters worse is Watters's penchant for revealing his less than rigorous research methodology: "I was searching the Web with words like 'friendship,' 'loyalty,' 'meaning of' and came across Aristotle's thought on the topic. Actually, it was not Aristotle's writing I found but rather a half-dozen student papers written about Aristotle. According to these trenchant scholars . . . Aristotle noodled a good deal on friendship."

New Rule: Friends don't let friends become pseudo-sociologists.

How obvious of an "epiphany" did Watters have? Really, there was no need to look any further than prime-time television to realize that nonfamilial relationships had become central to people's lives and that the traditional nuclear family was no longer *the* defining social configuration. From *Leave It to Beaver* and *All in the Family* to *Family Ties, The Cosby Show,* and *Growing Pains,* the nuclear family was clearly the predominant "situation" for comedy and/or drama until *Seinfeld* came along in 1989. It seems a bit ridiculous to point this out, but since the trend-story editors hadn't noticed that Watters's epiphany was all over television throughout the 1990s, here's to stating the obvious: shows had long been reflecting this friends "trend," from *Melrose Place* to *Friends* (?!) and *Sex and the City*. Even when familial relationships defined the characters, shows were hardly celebrating the love of family and instead tended toward the dysfunctional: *Married With Children, The Simpsons, Arrested Development*.

Rather than focusing on his Burning Man tribe, Watters would have had a much more robust trend to explore had he looked to the work space he cofounded with two friends/colleagues called Grotto, described as "an office for the creative self-employed, people who by definition don't need to punch a clock."[3] What started in a six-room flat in a run-down Victorian on Market Street in San Francisco has evolved into an important incubator for writers, filmmakers, and other culture producers who share inspiration and ideas—or just want to work "alone together." This is far more revealing about why these relationships have become so significant. As the Grotto website explains: "The original hypothesis—that community is conducive to productivity—has proven abundantly true. In the past twelve years a steady stream of books, articles, feature films, television series, short stories, poems and essays have had their genesis here."[4]

And this is precisely why friends, colleagues, and rich social networks have become so important: like golf course networking for corporate executives, contemporary professions are ever more dependent on these relationships. Not only do they take time to build, they also require social spaces in close proximity so people can interact. Even more significant, innovation and cultural production are extremely reliant on the spontaneous sharing of ideas and information in random, unscripted ways. As Elizabeth Currid documents in *The Warhol Economy*, "Creativity would not exist as successfully or efficiently without its social world. The social is not the by-product—it is the decisive mechanism by which cultural products and cultural producers are generated, evaluated and sent to the market."[5] As Currid's research shows, people working in technology innovation, arts, music, fashion, design, and media are far more likely to live and work in close proximity to each other than people in finance, medicine, law, and other "golf course" professions, which are still heavily dependent on the old boys' network method of doing business.

Of course, culture producers have always been dependent on one another, forming artist enclaves whether intentionally or not. As the singer-songwriter Steve Earle—who is a historian of the early folk scene in Greenwich Village, created by Bob Dylan, Joan Baez, and the like—told *The New Yorker* shortly after moving there from Nashville: "This is where they invented what I do. And it happened only because there were these three groups—folksingers, the musicologists, and the writers—who happened to be living in this several-block radius. If that scene doesn't happen, then rock and roll never becomes literature. It just stays pop."[6] Of course, technology has expanded the creative economy beyond the traditional arts and music scene. And the lines between "friend" and "colleague" have blurred considerably. Accordingly, these relationships have become critically important not just on a personal level, but on the level of the overall economy.[7]

Annie Price grew up in Vancouver, Washington, just outside Portland, Oregon. In high school and college she cultivated her singing voice, and after working for a couple of years as a TV reporter, quit her job to tour with a cover band. It was one of the most memorable times of her life, but she eventually ran out of money and went back to local TV reporting in Portland, where she worked until a friend and colleague told her about a job opening at the NBC affiliate in Nashville. Knowing of Annie's interest in music, particularly country music, and also having a good contact at the Nashville station, her friend suggested she apply for the job. She jumped. Not only did Annie find a job in Nashville, she landed in the middle of the thriving early 1990s country music scene. So even though her first job in Nashville at the television station was short-lived (the show was cancelled and she got laid off), she was there just long enough to connect with this community and quickly find another job with a small production company that covered the country music business.

"They had just invented SoundScan, which kept track of record sales, and everyone realized how underestimated country music sales had been. So this whole thing takes off, and with the entertainment business, so much business is conducted *during* entertainment. So I was in the middle of a big party scene. You play at this tennis round-robin, or go to this party or a showcase for some new artists. There was something going on every night of the week and people went to them. It was really fun. You did a lot of business with a beer in your hand at these parties.

"At this small production company, we had beats. I had Warner Brothers and Atlantic Records, and a few others. Faith Hill was just breaking. She started at a little office in Nashville. I did one of her first TV interviews. So this publicity agent at Warner Brothers asks me to produce a presentation for their annual meeting, and everyone thought it was great, so they offered me a video production job. So I produced a whole bunch of Faith Hill videos. I probably produced seventy-five music videos for Warner Brothers. Then Hootie and the Blowfish came out and country music just took a dive. I survived one round of layoffs, but not the second round. This was the beginning of a downhill economic spiral for me that lasted for quite a long time. That's when you find out who your friends are."

Annie's Warner Brothers contract was bought out, so she left Nashville for a year to study improv in Chicago, but eventually ran out of money (again) and returned to Nashville to start a business with a partner, which didn't go especially well. She wound up at Dell, selling computers over the phone, which is where she was on 9/11: "I was working the nightshift on September 11, and I didn't have to be in until 2:00 in the afternoon. My girlfriend called me at home and said some kind of a bomb has gone off and told me to turn on the TV. So I watched the towers fall and called Dell and they're like, 'Come in, business as usual.' I very clearly remember, you could tell the managers had been coached on what to say: 'It's a trying day, but we can't let commerce stop because it's the American way and the terrorists would win.' I'm like, what? It was completely crazy. There were TV monitors airing news reports, and they had an overlay of graphics showing how many calls were waiting, and the queue was full. I remember being astounded that people were calling and buying computers as if nothing had happened. So they were right; it was business as usual."

While hocking Dell computers for $12 an hour at the age of thirty-five, the former VP of video production for Warner Brothers (!) decided to go back to school—another common theme for Generation X.[8] She applied to the midcareer program at Columbia University's Graduate School of Journalism in New York, a small, yearlong master's degree for experienced journalists. (This program was nicknamed "the midcareer crisis program" by thirtysomething students.) From there, Annie moved to Chicago (with an additional $30,000 in debt), where once again she tapped one of her closest friends, Gail, whom she had worked with in Nashville, to help her get a job with the *Oprah* show. "I remember going to dinner with Gail and saying 'I'm really in trouble. Please help me get in the door.' At first she was like, 'It's such hard work, the hours are insane, all the traveling,' etc. She tried to discourage me. I was like, 'You see this Ahi tuna I'm eating? You're paying for it because I can't afford to pay for my own dinner.' I was like, 'You've got to get me in the door!' Gail walked my resume in."

After two years with *Oprah*, Annie is now in LA working as an independent director, doing commercials and television work, and she is about to shoot her first short film: "This is when the social network really comes into play. I just did this reality show, everyone on that show is like, 'What are you doing next? Oh, I know the producer on that, give me your resume,' etc. I'm about to head back to Chicago to make this short film, and I'm calling in every friend I have there. I'm filming there while *Oprah* is on hiatus because that's when everyone will be available. People are really stepping up to help me with this project. I'm bankrolling it myself and people know how much these things cost. I'm probably going to run out of money again. Good thing I'm with a corporate lawyer now. She's the best."

Although Annie's reliance on friends and her social network to get her through layoffs and wild income swings are consistent with current trends, surprisingly, all the moving around she has done turns out to be less common than conventional wisdom would have us believe. Just as technology was supposed to create the paperless office and render "place" meaningless, it is also widely assumed to have increased mobility. But people are less likely to move today than at any point since the Census Bureau started gathering mobility stats in 1948. In 2004 only 19 percent of all movers, or 3 percent of U.S. residents, moved to another state. Most moved within the same county. As would be expected, most movers are people in their twenties. And although highly educated people tend to move more, they aren't more likely to do so now than in the past.[9]

There are any number of explanations for decreasing locational mobility (such as increased homeownership), but one is certainly that professional development has become intertwined with rich social networks. These networks, despite being facilitated by electronic communication, tend to be very place-specific. As Annie would attest, pulling up stakes mid-career to start all over again is very difficult—and probably not usually undertaken willingly. The longer people stay in one place, the more friendships and networks they are able to expand and deepen, making it ever more difficult to re-create that elsewhere. Annie, too, assumed that people moved around as much as she did, but upon reflection realized that most people she knows in her industry are located in New York or LA and, other than traveling a lot, aren't necessarily making major moves very often.

Despite so much evidence to the contrary, researchers and social scientists are still inclined to believe that technology has fragmented relationships, increased mobility, and caused social isolation. The authors of "Social Isolation in America: Changes in Core Discussion Networks over Two Decades" reported with alarm that the number of close friends people claim to have has decreased from about three in 1985 to two in 2004, and that people were less likely to have a close confidant outside their immediate family.[10] But Ann Hulburt, writing for the *New York Times Sunday* magazine, had a different take:

> [B]efore rushing to conclude that Americans have simply gotten lonelier and more insular, why not consider another possibility? Perhaps, as the study's authors themselves hint at one point, we've also gotten better at demarcating what constitutes truly intimate communing—expecting more of our confidants, we have, in effect, defined intimacy up.[11]

Contrary to the Luddite tendency to believe that technology is an isolating force, a study by the Pew Internet and American Life Project concluded that technology had greatly expanded social networks. People reported a median of fifteen "core" and sixteen "significant" ties; much of this expanded circle is facilitated by e-mail and the Internet, which *have not* supplanted other forms of contact.[12] Social isolation is hardly the issue, lending support to the idea that discerning who is truly a confidant from this large of a group does require a more exacting definition of intimacy.

So although Watters seemed to recognize something significant was going on with adult friendships, he misread the causes and effects. It's not that friendship was replacing marriage, it was that friendships and social ties have become increasingly important for professional development, idea exchange, innovation, and creativity. Ironically, Po Bronson, a cofounder with Watters of the San Francisco work space Grotto, has exhaustively documented the current state of the American family experience, and he reports that more than 90 percent of Americans will marry at some point in their lives.[13] In other words, Watters had it exactly wrong. Friends had *not* become the new family, and, in fact, Watters himself married before he even finished his book.

But Watters did manage to make one good observation in his critique of Robert Putnam's book *Bowling Alone*. Even though it was a stats-laden lamentation on the demise of traditional community, Putnam did briefly notice that friendships had actually strengthened. However, since this didn't fit with his overall thesis that communities are falling apart, he merely made a note of it, then let it drop: "Twentieth century urbanization was not fatal to friendship. Urban settings sustain not a single tightly integrated community, but a mosaic of loosely coupled communities . . . friendship may actually have gained importance in the modern metropolis."[14]

Of this, Watters notes in *Urban Tribes*: "It was an intriguing insight, to say the least, but unfortunately he didn't head in the direction it pointed. . . . It was as if he had seen the urban tribe out of the corner of his eye but failed to turn and take a close look."[15] Watters, on the other hand, did turn to take a closer look, but unfortunately failed to see it clearly. Perhaps it was the thick smoke of Burning Man obscuring his vision.

9

Love: Is It Real or Is It Memorex?

Before Sunrise (1995)
Richard Linklater (director)
Jesse (Ethan Hawke)
Céline (Julie Delpy)

Opening Scene

EURAIL COACH CAR. DAY

Baby-boomer-aged man and woman argue in German. Woman slaps man, grabs newspaper.

Céline looks up from book, disturbed. Moves to another seat, across from Jesse. They glance over at each other.

German woman leaves car in a huff.

Jesse and Céline look at each other, smile.

JESSE

Do you have any idea what they were arguing about? Do you—do you speak English?

CÉLINE

Yeah. No, I'm sorry, my German is not very good.

Have you ever heard that as couples get older, they lose their ability to hear each other?

JESSE

No.

CÉLINE

Well, supposedly, men lose the ability to hear higher-pitched sounds, and women eventually lose hearing in the low end. I guess they sort of nullify each other, or something.

JESSE

I guess. Nature's way of allowing couples to grow old together without killing each other.

So opens *Before Sunrise*, perhaps the first of a new film subgenre—call it the unsentimental romance movie. Coupled with its sequel, *Before Sunset*, released nine years later, no two films better capture this generation's love-hate relationship with modern romance and marriage. Hailed by critics and audiences alike, ReelViews movie critic James Berardinelli (born in 1967 in Morristown, New Jersey) called *Before Sunrise* "the best romance of all time."[1] Yet unlike most great romantic movies, like *Gone With the Wind* or *Love Story*, there is virtually no melodrama, quite a bit of ambivalence, very little plot, and few characters other than Jesse and Céline, who get off the train together in Vienna, from where Jesse has a ticket to fly back to the United States the next morning. Without enough money to rent a hotel room for the night, the two walk and talk their way around the city, philosophizing about everything from the pursuit of happiness to the existence of God, but most of all about love and the viability of long-term, committed relationships.

Of course, great love stories, requited and unrequited, hinge on sexual tension, not intellectual masturbation. For previous generations of moviemakers, that tension usually revolved around sexual taboos, such as premarital sex (*Splendor in the Grass*) or infidelity (*Casablanca*). One of the more recent critically acclaimed love stories, *Brokeback Mountain*, had to reach back in time in order to create an unabashedly sentimental romance around the taboo of love and sex between two men. By the time Gen X came of age, however, most taboos had been broken, so the tension in *Before Sunrise* comes from having witnessed the breakdown of love-based marriage and the resulting mistrust of emotional vulnerability, i.e., romantic love. But of course, people are hardwired for sexual attraction and love, so even a healthy bit of skepticism can't stop a great affair, even if it only lasts for a night.

The train reaches Jesse's stop. After getting his bag, he heads back to the dining car table where he just said good-bye to Céline and tries to convince her to join him for a day—and night—in Vienna.

JESSE

Alright, think of it like this: jump ahead ten, twenty years, okay? And you're married. Only your marriage doesn't have that same energy that it used to have, you know? You start to blame your husband. You start to think of all those guys you met in your life and what might have happened if you'd picked up with one of them, right? Well I'm one of those guys, that's me!

So think of this as time travel. From then to now to find out what you're missing out on. See, what this really could be is a gigantic favor to both you and your future husband to find out that you're not missing out on anything; I'm just as big a loser as he is, totally unmotivated, totally boring, and you made the right choice and you're really happy.

CÉLINE

(*thinking for a moment*)
Let me get my bag.

Once again Generation X found itself bridging a cavernous gap caused by economic shifts, in this case between the 300-year-old notion that people married for love to the realization that love is an inherently unstable basis for a long-term committed relationship. As social historian Stephanie Coontz exhaustively documents in the book *Marriage, a History: From Obedience to Intimacy, or How Love Conquered Marriage*, for 5,000 years marriage had been primarily an economic relationship—until the onset of the Industrial Revolution:

> During the eighteenth century the spread of the market economy and the advent of the Enlightenment wrought profound changes in record time. By the end of the 1700s personal choice of partners had replaced arranged marriage as a social ideal, and individuals were encouraged to marry for love. . . . The measure of a successful marriage was no longer how big a financial settlement was involved, how many useful in-laws were acquired, or how many children were produced, but how well a family met the emotional needs of its individual members.[2]

The love match was on.

But that all came apart less than 300 years later when baby-boomer women demanded economic parity and joined the workforce in unprecedented numbers. As couples fell out of love—which of course they had always done before, but weren't so readily able to act on it—divorce rates soared. Gen Xers grew up when marriages were crumbling in unprecedented numbers.[3] Consequently, as they reached traditional marrying age, they were left to figure out for themselves the next iteration of an institution that had for centuries been the primary social organizing relationship.

"Today we are experiencing a historical revolution every bit as wrenching, far-reaching, and irreversible as the Industrial Revolution," wrote Coontz. "Like that huge historic turning point, the revolution in marriage has transformed how people organize their work and interpersonal commitments, use their leisure time, understand their sexuality, and take care of children and the elderly. It has liberated some people from restrictive, inherited roles in society. But it has stripped others of traditional support systems and rules of behavior without establishing new ones."[4]

Needless to say, this has created a bit of confusion and skepticism about the connection between romantic love and long-term commitment. But that is not to say that romance ceased to exist. Evolutionary biologists have long theorized that attraction has a profoundly deep-seated biological basis, evolved to bring people together to procreate. Interestingly, the brain scans of gay men and women in the grip of love look the same as straight couples.[5] Consequently, although attraction and romance are hardwired to compel procreation, the mind doesn't make that connection. And that in fact may be part of the evolutionary adaptation: if there was a hardwired link between sexual attraction and babies, people might work harder to avoid it when procreation was not on the agenda. Of course, people do consciously understand that relationship between sexual attraction and procreation, but although sexual desire and romantic love have proven to be mighty powerful instincts, the widespread use of birth control and the availability of abortion in the industrialized world have all but completely severed uncontrollable, ill-considered passion from resulting procreation. Since couples are no longer bound by procreation or economic necessity, making the transition from romantic love to a long-term commitment has become increasingly difficult.

The sun has set and Céline and Jesse are walking through The Prater, a famous amusement park in Vienna, having just taken a ride on a Ferris wheel where they kiss for the first time.

CÉLINE

You know, I've been wondering lately. Do you know anyone who's in a happy relationship?

JESSE

Uh, yeah, sure, I know happy couples. But I think they lie to each other.

CÉLINE

Yeah. People can lead their life as a lie. My grandmother, she was married to this man, and I always thought she had a very simple, uncomplicated love life. But she just confessed to me that she spent her whole life dreaming about another man she was always in love with. She just accepted her fate. It's so sad. . . .

JESSE

I guarantee you, it was better that way. If she'd ever got to know him, you know, I'm sure he would have disappointed her eventually.

CÉLINE

How do you know? You don't know them.

JESSE

Yeah, I know, I know. It's just, people have these romantic projections they put on everything. You know, that's not based on any kind of reality.

CÉLINE

Romantic projections?

JESSE

Yeah.

CÉLINE

Oh, Mr. Romantic, up there in the Ferris wheel "Oh, kiss me, the sunset, oh, it's so beautiful . . . "

JESSE

Oh, alright, alright. Tell me about your grandmother. What were you saying about her?

Making matters worse (or better, depending on your point of view), technological advances of the past twenty years allow us to study previously unstudyable things at the biological and chemical level, such as sexual attraction, romantic love, and long-term commitment. Much like a magician revealing the mechanics of a trick, pulling back the curtain on the wondrously enthralling human condition called love can be both revelatory and disillusioning. And, as it turns out, sexual attraction, romantic love, and long-term commitment are—albeit with some overlap—pretty distinct phenomena that can be experienced with different people at the same time.[6] So let's start with the first: sexual attraction.

In his book *Consilience: The Unity of Knowledge*, evolutionary biologist Edward O. Wilson explains the *supernormal stimulus*—widespread among animal species—as the preference for exaggerated signals that rarely if ever occur in nature. Researchers discovered that they could mimic the silver-dappled orange butterfly with plastic replicas to attract males during breeding season. "To their surprise," Wilson writes, "[researchers] learned that males turn from real females and fly toward the models that have the biggest, brightest, and most rapidly moving wings. No such superfemale exists in the species' natural environment. Males . . . appear to have evolved to prefer the strongest expression of certain stimuli they encounter, with no upper limit." Dr. Wilson concludes that for humans, "the entire beauty industry can be interpreted as the manufacture of supernormal stimuli,"[7] which in humans may be better termed the *Pamela Anderson syndrome*.

Sexual attraction and romantic love, however, are two different things, according to research conducted by Dr. Helen Fisher, an anthropologist and author of *Why We Love: The Nature and Chemistry of Romantic Love*. While sexual attraction in humans is largely driven by testosterone (in both men and women), romantic love compels people to choose a particular mate rather than merely deriving pleasure from random sexual encounters. Although humans are increasingly enjoying random hookups, thanks in part to the Internet, romantic love is in no danger of disappearing anytime soon. Largely controlled by the hormones dopamine, norepinephrine, and serotonin—and equally strong in men and women—it is an instinct more powerful than hunger.[8]

Furthermore, not only are lust and love driven by different hormones, they are also associated with different regions of the brain. The good news is that the love hormones can stimulate the lust hormone (testosterone), but it doesn't work in the other direction: testosterone does not induce the love hormones. This condition had previously been thought of as experienced by men almost exclusively, but as sexual norms have loosened, it has become clear that women are just as capable of engaging in emotionally detached sexual relationships. What's more, not only does sex not necessarily lead to love, romantic love is short-lived and not very stable. The latest research indicates that romantic love lasts about three years before fizzling out,[9] which means it is not a great basis for long-term commitment and/or childrearing.

It all seems rather cruel. The very drives that bring people together, both sexual and romantic, don't necessarily translate into long-term attachment, which is driven by an entirely different set of hormones. Humans and a few other monogamous species experience attachment hormones—oxytocin and vasopressin—which are also known as the "cuddle chemicals." Not only do these hormones play a role in adult long-term attachment, in women oxytocin bonds mothers to children and reduces testosterone in men. In fact, with the birth of a child, men experience a significant decline in testosterone. Not only do the attachment hormones reduce the lust hormones for both men and women, they also dampen the brain chemistry of romantic love. And therein lies the rub.

Although humans are monogamous, as with all things evolutionary, there is variation. It has been observed that other monogamous species do cheat, which is directly related to how many or how few receptors a particular brain has for the attachment hormones.[10] But by and large, monogamy and long-term attachment are not achieved via the hormones that correspond to romantic love, which can be experienced extemporaneously while still feeling long-term attachment with a partner. It is no wonder then that marriage and familial relationships were more tightly bound when economic survival largely depended on it, rather than the longevity of love and attraction.

But this is not to say that economics doesn't still play a major role in the institution of marriage. According to Coontz, the increasingly volatile and changing economy continues to have profound effects on expectations of long-term commitment. She states:

> [T]he end of the 1970s saw the dawn of a different kind of insecurity. A churning global economy wiped out old jobs and entire industries, but opened up tempting new opportunities in different arenas, then shifted again suddenly. This constantly changing economic and technological environment forced people to move away from conventional scripts

for behavior. . . . [M]en and women had to maximize their individual freedom of action and keep their options open. . . . All these changes led to new tensions between men and women.[11]

Céline and Jesse are walking through an alleyway.

CÉLINE

No, no, no, wait a minute. Talking seriously here. I mean, I always feel this pressure of being a strong and independent icon of womanhood, and without making, making it look like my whole life is revolving around some guy. But loving someone, and being loved means so much to me. We always make fun of it and stuff. But isn't everything we do in life a way to be loved a little more?

They sit on a bench.

JESSE

Yeah, I don't know. Sometimes I dream about being a good father and a good husband, and sometimes that feels really close. But then, other times, it seems silly, like it would ruin my whole life. And it's not just a fear of commitment, or that I'm incapable of caring, or loving, because I can. It's just that if I'm totally honest with myself, I think I'd rather die knowing that I was really good at something, that I had excelled in some way, you know, than that I had just been in a nice, caring relationship.

But as every great romance story reveals, neither social taboos nor scientific rationality can overcome the pull of a great affair. It seems when it comes to love, the old saw "once bitten, twice shy" doesn't apply. Perhaps "once bitten, twice smitten" is more like it.

The sun has not yet risen. Céline and Jesse are lying together in a park drinking a bottle of red wine, debating whether or not to consummate their love affair, and if they should try to see each other again.

CÉLINE

Now let's just be rational adults about this. We, maybe we should try something different. I mean, it's not so bad if tonight is our only night, right? People always exchange phone numbers, addresses, they end up writing once, calling each other once or twice . . .

JESSE

Right. Fizzles out. Yeah, I mean, I don't want that. I hate that.

CÉLINE

I hate that too, you know.

JESSE

Why do you think everybody thinks relationships are supposed to last forever?

CÉLINE

Yeah, why. It's stupid.

JESSE

So, you think tonight's it, huh? I mean, that, tonight's our only night.

CÉLINE

It's the only way, no?

JESSE

Well, alright. Let's do it. No delusions, no projections. We'll just make tonight great.

CÉLINE

Okay, let's do that.

JESSE

. . . Listen, if somebody gave me the choice right now, of to never see you again or to marry you, alright, I would marry you. And maybe that's a lot of romantic bullshit, but people have gotten married for a lot less.

Céline and Jesse allow themselves to have their great night, part ways with a plan to meet back in Vienna in six months, but don't do anything foolish like get married at the tender age of twentysomething. In fact, they don't even exchange contact information. In the sequel, *Before Sunset*, we learn that their meeting in Vienna six months later goes awry, and it takes nine more years before they encounter each other again in Paris. In another era, they may very well have eloped that night, or at least made more concrete plans for the future. But their skepticism about the longevity of romantic relationships—coupled with the unspoken pressures of not yet having careers or even having finished school—stops the young lovers from making promises they can't keep.

Social commentators have lamented the fact that Generation X began "delaying marriage" or eschewing it altogether, and, indeed, by 2005 single women outnumbered married women,[12] and by 2006 people in traditional marriages were in the minority for the first time in American history.[13] But if 90 percent of the population gets married at some point in their lives, is marriage really in decline? And if people who could very well live to be a hundred years old aren't getting married until their thirties and later, is this really "delaying" marriage? "The dramatic extension of adults' life expectancy since 1970 has also changed the terms of marriage," Coontz writes. "An American who reaches age sixty today can expect to live another twenty-five years. The average married couple will live for more than three decades after their kids have left home. . . . *No previous generation has ever been asked to make such a long-term commitment.*"[14]

Grant Marquit—smart and energetic, with wide-ranging interests and a penchant for spot-on imitations—grew up in a largely Jewish suburb of Cleveland with two older sisters and one younger one. Like many of his neighborhood friends, his parents divorced when he was very young: "In the 1970s, it seemed like everyone was getting divorced, especially in the liberal Jewish community." Grant's early experience of seeing so many marriages dissolve—as well as the scientific knowledge about biological compatibility—shaped his viewpoint about love and marriage into what might be called practical romanticism.

"When I first started understanding relationships, I thought it was all about love. And I remember being in love. And that's all nice, but we also know that we fall out of love. It's not to say those relationships aren't important; you're pushing the limits of the relationship to help yourself grow. But there's something very selfish about it. So I really started to break it all down. Since high school, I knew I wanted kids, and I didn't want to adopt or be a single parent, so I knew I needed a woman and that she had to have a shelf life of twenty years, at least. I would have to be able to tolerate this person for a long time.

"So the first thing, I knew I wanted to choose someone with good genes, and I mean that seriously. I studied biology in college and I knew there was this strong genetic component to the raising of healthy, well-adjusted kids. The whole nature versus nurture debate had swung toward nature, and it was really in the popular culture at the time, too. I remember my sister Marla saying, 'Forget about beautiful women, they're a dime a dozen.' I was like, 'Okay, here's a dollar, let me pick from the first 120 and go from there.' Smart people are a little more expensive.

"As I had relationships I realized good genes was just the start. There had to be certain characteristics, some seem really stupid and shallow but they matter. With one girlfriend, she had all these allergies and asthma. Maybe that was a natural selection thing, but we couldn't go hiking and ride bikes. That bothered me. Another thing, I like to dance. I want to be with someone who is going to get up there and boogie down. So the self-conscious, shy-girl thing didn't work for me. Also, I couldn't deal with someone who needed a lot of money. I make a decent living, but that's never been my motivation. I love to cook and eat different kinds of food; if that person wasn't into trying new things, it ain't gonna work. Can't have a lot of food issues. Another thing I realized, they couldn't be a jealous person. I grew up with all women. I love women. I have a couple guy friends, but most of my friends are women.

"So every relationship post-college got progressively shorter. I learned, maybe because I had gained maturity, to start paying attention a little sooner. I knew what I wanted—kids and a wife—so let's stop fucking around. It got to the point where I had several no-strings-attached-type relationships, but I just was not going to get involved in a long-term thing unless certain criteria were met. What's the point? So the people I dated were in and out pretty quick. Three dates, and out.

"Then technology came into the picture. You could kind of check off these boxes and hopefully find someone. So in 1998, 1999, I was like, okay, I've never had a Jewish girlfriend, so I'm going to check these boxes and find a great Jewish girl. Well, it doesn't quite work that way, either.

"So Amy, my wife, thank god for wine, she was all drunk, out with her friends, couples were dancing; it was a Latin band. I was kind of moving my feet in the corner, not on the dance floor yet. So this Amy walks up and asks me to dance. I was like, yeah! As it turned out, five minutes later, we realized we knew each other in high school. Here was somebody who swept me onto the dance floor—literally, she's taller than me—and then called me the next day, and said, 'Hey, let's go out!'

"We go out on our first date, and I know Amy is not a no-strings-attached kind of person. So I was like, 'Look, I want kids and a wife. I'm not doing this long-term relationship thing unless we meet certain criteria.' And by the way, at this point, falling in love was like third or fourth on my list. The things that were important were good genes, similar value system, and chemistry, which is different from dreamy-eyed love. Love is totally emotional; chemistry is physical. This dreamy-eyed stuff always fades. People in love do stupid shit. They don't see what's right in front of their faces. So I said, 'I'm not looking for a long-term thing unless we're really serious.' She totally understood what I was saying.

"After two weeks, three or four dates, I was like, 'This is going pretty well. Let me run something by you: let's reevaluate this every now and then, check out our emotions so we can be as rational as we can be.' Now we're at six months, and I suggest we go to a counselor, and say, 'We're thinking that we're going to have a committed relationship, but we need someone to help make us aware of our blind spots in terms of compatibility.'" Under the guidance of their counselor, Grant and Amy both took the Minnesota Multiphasic Personality Inventory (MMPI), an in-depth personality and mental health test. They were deemed more or less compatible, got married less than a year later, and at the time of our interview, Grand and Amy had two kids and another on the way.

"It's not perfect, but for what my goals were, it totally worked. I've got beautiful kids. I have a smart wife. She's got a career, so she's not dependent on me in that way. The chemistry is there. So I know even when I fucking hate her, which does happen, I know that when I crawl back into bed, my body starts doing the talking. So I never have a hard time having a hard time.

"Have I ever been dreamy-eyed about Amy? If I had to pick yes or no, I would say no. When I look at photographs of us together, just candid shots of us, we look like people who are in love, like two happy people. We're even starting to look alike. But this notion of in-love, what does that mean? You have a crush? Does it mean, they take your breath away? That never lasts. That is so temporal. I love that line by Krusty the Clown, 'It's not just good—it's good enough!'"

Grant and Amy were both in their thirties when they got married, and although age is of course no guarantee of wisdom, it certainly helps, and it may explain the growing trend of unsentimental or practical romanticism engendered by Generation X. And that in turn may help explain a drop in divorce rates as Generation X has moved into marrying age; there has been a statistically significant increase in a couple's chance of staying together, starting in the 1990s.[15] It might not be quite so romantic, but understanding the difference between dreamy-eyed romance, as Grant calls it, and long-term attachment could very well make the difference between picking the right person for a committed relationship and preventing foolish mistakes—from marrying too young to divorcing a spouse for an indiscretion.

Although marriage will likely never return to its previous configuration as primarily a financial/working relationship—the love genie won't ever be put back in the bottle completely—economics are once again playing a role in keeping people together. Unlike for the baby-boomers, where increasing economic independence for women destabilized love-based marriage, now Generation X is motivated not to get hitched too young. This motivation is prompted by a need not only to be better established financially before marriage, but also—as the likelihood of experiencing wild income swings has increased and thus having another income-earner in the house can help smooth over the rough patches—to find someone with whom one can stick it out for the long haul. What's more, a married couple living in a household that earns $50,000 a year or better is significantly more likely to stay together,[16] a clear indication that economics can be a deciding factor whether or not people are even *able* to stick together. But that alone, however, will not keep people married. As the economists might say, increased stability from sharing the financial burden is a necessary but not sufficient condition for a commitment to last.

In *Before Sunset*, released in 2004, Jesse and Céline meet again, this time in Paris. Jesse has written a thinly disguised autobiographical novel about his one great romantic encounter in Vienna. On the last leg of a promotional tour, he is speaking at a bookstore in Paris where Céline lives. She shows up at the tail end of the question-and-answer period, but instead of running toward each other, arms outstretched like a slo-mo beach scene, they approach each other with a mixture of anticipation and trepidation, now even more reluctant to reveal too much emotion. As the two walk and talk their way around Paris, much as they did in Vienna, we learn that Jesse is in a passionless marriage with a girlfriend he knocked up, and Céline has had a series of less than satisfying relationships. She chooses to be with people—such as her current boyfriend, an international photographer—who don't suffocate her or impinge on her independence.

On a touristy boat along the Seine, Jesse and Céline slowly begin to talk more openly about their lives.

CÉLINE

What is it like to be married? You haven't talked much about that.

JESSE

I haven't? How weird. We met when I was in college. We broke up, got back together. Then we were sort of back together, she got pregnant, so marriage. She's a great teacher, good mom. She's smart, pretty. I remember thinking at the time, so many of the men I admire the most, their lives were dedicated to something greater than themselves.

. . . I have this idea of my best self, and I wanted to pursue that even if that was overriding my honest self. In the moment, I remember thinking the "who" of it all didn't much matter, it was about committing yourself and meeting your responsibilities. No one is going to be everything. What is love? Respect, trust, admiration. I felt all those things. Cut to the present tense, I feel like I'm running a small nursery with someone I used to date. I'm like a monk. I've had sex less than ten times in four years. . . . Okay I'm doing better than most monks, but I feel like if someone were to touch me I would dissolve into molecules.

Jesse and Céline get off the boat and are waiting for Jesse's driver to pick him up to go to the airport.

CÉLINE

Well, this friend of mine, she's a shrink, and . . . she was telling me that she's been dealing with a lot of couples that are breaking up for the same exact reason . . . all these couples expected, after a few years of living together, for the passion, that consuming desire, to be the same as in the beginning. It's impossible! I mean, God, otherwise we would end up with an aneurism if we were in that constant state of excitement, right? We would end up doing nothing at all with our lives.

Do you think you would have finished your book, if—

JESSE

—if I were fucking somebody every five minutes? I might have welcomed the challenge.

CÉLINE

. . . You know, couples are so confused lately. I think it must be that men need to feel essential, and they don't anymore. Because it's been imprinted in their heads, for so many years, that they had to be the provider. Like I, I'm a strong independent woman in my professional life. I don't need a man to feed me, but I still need a man to love me, and that I could love, you know?

The driver arrives, and Jesse offers to give Céline a ride home. They get in the car and continue talking.

CÉLINE

I was thinking, for me it's better I don't romanticize things as much anymore. I was suffering so much all the time. I still have lots of dreams, but they're not in regard to my love life. It doesn't make me sad, it's just the way it is. . . .

For all her rationality, Céline finally begins to crack:

You know . . . I was fine until I read your fucking book! It stirred shit up. It reminded me how genuinely romantic I was, how I had so much hope in things and now it's like I don't believe in anything that relates to love, I don't feel things for people anymore. In a way, I put all my romanticism into that one night and I was never able to feel all this again. . . .

JESSE

I am, I'm so glad you didn't forget about me.

CÉLINE

No, I didn't and it pisses me off, ok? You come here to Paris, all romantic, and married. Ok? Screw you! Don't get me wrong, I'm not trying to get you, or anything. I mean, all I need is a married man! There's been so much water under the bridge, it's, it's not even about you anymore, it's about that time, that moment in time, that is forever gone.

Like the first film, the movie ends on an ambiguous note. Jesse deliberately misses his plane and is clearly going to spend the night with Céline, but the consequences are left unknown. Do they share just one more night and go back to their more responsible lives? Or, in a kind of reverse psychology, do they throw all caution to the wind in a way that they were unable to do in their younger days? Do they take a more pragmatic approach by doing their best to deal appropriately with their individual relationships in hopes of pursuing a real life together? Do they marry or cohabitate? Do they have a child of their own? *Can it last?*

Like everything else for Generation X, the uncertainty is both the bad and the good news. As Coontz concluded her seminal book on the history of marriage:

> The bad news is that the institution of marriage will never again be as universal or stable as it was when marriage was the only viable option. But that is also the good news. . . . The same personal freedoms that allow people to expect more from their married lives also allow them to get more out of staying single and give them more choice than ever before in history about whether or not to remain together.[17]

10

The Breeders

Sex and the City, arguably the most culturally significant television show at the turn of the century, was, of course, about not just sex, but also the myriad social configurations that have emerged, particularly in a city where the possibilities are endless yet the choices still somehow seem inadequate. The show became famous for its no-holds-barred discussion of sex, but that now seems rather tame in comparison to what would later proliferate on the Internet. What is still relevant from this show are the characters and story lines, in large part because the show successfully managed to straddle a very difficult divide. The series, based on a column in the *New York Observer* by Candace Bushnell, was conceived during the bubble years, when the biggest issue in America was a presidential blow job that precipitated a constitutional crisis. Yet the series concluded in 2004—a time when the world had become a whole lot more complicated than scoring a pair of Manolo Blahniks or a hottie for a one-night stand. The blithe pursuit of hedonistic pleasures that characterized the first part of the series no longer seemed appropriate in post-9/11 America, which had been rudely awakened from its food coma by a massive failure to connect the dots.

Of course, a television program called *Sex and the City* was not going to morph into a cultural critique of geopolitical strife, but, nonetheless, dots needed to be connected if the show was to stay relevant. Indeed, the oftentimes surprising relationship between sex and procreation emerged as a major theme in the latter half of the series. In the fourth season, Charlotte is married and confronting the fact that she can't conceive, while in the same episode Samantha and Carrie admit to having had abortions in the context of Miranda's unplanned pregnancy. Miranda, the sarcastic Harvard-educated corporate lawyer, had "sympathy sex" with her on-again, off-again boyfriend Steve (an underachieving but lovable bartender), who recently had one ball removed because of testicular cancer. She tells Carrie about her unwanted pregnancy, lamenting the fact that they didn't use birth control.

MIRANDA

Why didn't I use a condom?!

CARRIE

You didn't use a condom?

MIRANDA

He has one ball, and I have a lazy ovary! In what twisted world does that create a baby? It's like the Special Olympics of conception.

At first, Miranda is not going to tell Steve and wants to quietly end the pregnancy, but since no one on television or in the movies is allowed to have an abortion, she ultimately decides to keep the baby.

Oh, how times have changed. Not even Dick Cheney would have the balls to launch an attack on popular culture for debasing family values the way Dan Quayle did when Murphy Brown was in a similar situation a decade earlier: "It doesn't help matters when primetime TV has Murphy Brown—a character who supposedly epitomizes today's intelligent, highly paid, professional woman—mocking the importance of a father by bearing a child alone and calling it just another 'lifestyle choice.'" In fact, Cheney's own lesbian daughter conceived a child with a sperm donor and is raising it with her longtime companion. (One wonders if Dan Quayle would have the temerity to criticize Mary Cheney for mocking the importance of a father, given the Veep's penchant for shooting his own friends in the face.)

At no time in history have there been more options for getting pregnant and raising kids, and Generation X seems to be taking advantage of them all. Once upon a time "test tube" babies and surrogate mothers were fodder for Movie-of-the-Week horror stories. Now there's gay adoption, in vitro fertilization, infertility treatments resulting in multiple births, conceiving children at the age of forty or later, donor eggs, single mothers by choice, Alternadads, and any number of family configurations in addition to the traditional kind. Of course, getting knocked up, as Miranda did, is nothing new.

But until very recently, the options were to get married, give it up for adoption, or have an illegal abortion.

Miranda eventually winds up where many people have before her: marrying the father of her child and embracing family life—although it is a circuitous route. She goes through her pregnancy as a single woman. ("The fat ass, the farting, it's ridiculous! I am unfuckable and I have never been so horny in my entire life. That's why you're supposed to be married when you're pregnant—so somebody is obligated to have sex with you!") Steve is at their son's delivery, and they share custody (only because Steve wants to be involved, not because Miranda required him to be), but they live apart and have relationships with other people. After a year of unconventional parenthood, they again become involved as a couple and cohabitate for a stint before getting married. (Miranda snaps at a sales clerk who is showing her a few potential wedding dresses while she is on her lunch break: "I said, 'No white, no ivory, nothing that says 'virgin.' I have a child. The jig is up.") Eventually Miranda, Steve, baby, and dog move from Manhattan to a brownstone in Brooklyn, but not everything about this arrangement is traditional. Miranda is still the major breadwinner and Steve is doing a lot of the domestic work. This neo-traditional approach to family, like so many other aspects of life for the post-boomer generation, means reinterpreting the instrumentation of a very old song.

Shifting economic circumstances (that phrase is starting to get repetitive, but hey, that's what the book is about . . .) changed family dynamics as they were previously understood just as Generation X began entering the traditional marrying years. As women's financial independence evolved from being revolutionary to assumed, and men's real wages stagnated, raising children outside of a traditional family configuration has become more practicable. This alteration of practice has, in turn, forever altered attitudes about the relationship between marriage and childbearing. Only 41 percent of Americans now say that children are "very important" to a successful marriage, a sharp downturn from the 65 percent who said this in a 1990 survey by the Pew Research Center. Children had been ranked third, but are now number eight out of nine on a list of items that people associate with successful marriages, including "sharing household chores," "good housing," "adequate income," "happy sexual relationship," and "faithfulness." The Pew survey also found that Americans believe the main purpose of marriage is the couple's "mutual happiness and fulfillment" rather than the "bearing and raising of children" by a margin of nearly three to one.

But that is not to say children are no longer important to parents. When asked to rank various relationships, parents rank children just as high as spouses and more important than their own parents, friends, jobs, or career. In fact, unwed parents say their children are the *most* important relationships in their lives. At the same time, the decline in traditional marriage is driving the "sharp growth in non-marital childbearing," not by unwed teenagers, which has been declining for years, but rather by "the increasing number of older women who are forgoing marriage but electing to have children."[1]

Leslie Hill—an attractive, soft-spoken chemist for an environmental consulting firm in Fort Collins, Colorado, a small town about an hour and a half north of Denver—began trying to get pregnant with her second husband, Peter, in 1998. They started simply enough by not using birth control: "Absolutely all of our education had been about preventing pregnancy. I knew nothing about getting pregnant. I didn't even know when you ovulate. How can you tell? So the first thing was figuring that out. When I wasn't getting pregnant right away, we did all the low-tech, over-the-counter stuff, ovulation prediction, etc. At some point I said to my GYN during my annual, 'I'm not having any luck here.' So they ordered a sperm count, and that was fine.

"After a while, I made the switch to a reproductive endocrinologist, a fertility specialist. You start with IUI's [intra-uterine insemination], where they wash the sperm and stick it up in there—just helping it get where it needs to go. Eventually I did IVF [in vitro fertilization] twice, taking fertility drugs, injectables, and a small surgery to retrieve eggs. They fertilize the eggs in the lab and put them back in. That's like $12,000 for each cycle. One was covered by insurance, which is amazing. Nobody has that kind of coverage. I paid for the other one out of pocket. Nothing happened. It was all pretty unexplained. There was never a diagnosis really as to why I couldn't get pregnant. We tried for seven years total. So when Peter and I split up—which was hugely related to this—I just felt like my body didn't work and I didn't know why. All the fertility issues were supposedly mine, but I felt like he's an asshole who couldn't deal with it. There's adoption and other options, but you have to have two people who are willing to do that, and he never was. When we split up, I was forty years old, so I thought I was never going to get pregnant.

"It's bewildering to be single at forty, and pretty depressing. But I started dating, first this old grad school friend of mine—it was a long distance relationship and we didn't use any birth control the whole time. Who knows what that was about. We saw each other probably twice a month, so maybe the timing was never right.

"Then I started dating Ken. We had known each other for a long time, having worked together for six or seven years. We were both hanging out with this other friend of ours from work who lives about an hour away. So we spent all this time driving down there together and spending the weekend with our friend. Finally on this camping trip, we got all liquored up and slept in the same tent and then started dating. It was very low-key; we were just having a good time. Peter and I were still in divorce mediation. And Ken is—I had always thought, you know how pretty boys are usually assholes? I thought he must secretly be an asshole. So I never really considered dating him before that camping trip.

"But we started going to shows, going to dinner, having lots of great sex, but we're still not telling anyone at work and keeping it low-key. Four months into it, I'm five days late, but I didn't think it was even possible. I just thought maybe my cycle got messed up. At this point, I'm forty-one, so maybe it was the beginnings of menopause or something. Who knows. We were about to take a shower, and I peed on this stick just to check, and I was like, 'You might want to see this.' We were like, 'Oh my god.' I went immediately to the doctor. I work in a lab, so God knows I didn't trust that stick.

"There were a couple of weeks of waiting to see if it was real, and then in one incredibly stunned moment we saw the heartbeat on ultrasound. We couldn't go back to work after that. Don't ever secretly date someone at work in case you get knocked up. It's very awkward. People were just starting to find out that Peter and I weren't together and next thing you know I'm hugely pregnant, and eventually you have to tell people who the dad is.

"I never really considered ending the pregnancy. We both want kids. Right off the bat Ken said, 'If we really didn't want this we would have used birth control.' We talked about kids early on and I told him that my only hope is donor eggs or adoption. I thought that's what we would try somewhere down the road, *way* down the road, if things worked out. But our relationship wasn't at a serious stage yet. I liked him a lot. I had just bought a house. I didn't know, but the month I got pregnant I signed the contract. We had discussed living together in the house before we found out. Ken was kind of like, 'I don't know yet.' I'm eight and a half months along and he just moved in two weeks ago.

"Do people even need to be married? In my mind, being married is ideal. But it just hasn't worked out that way for me. I just don't feel the need to rush into that after having been through two divorces. We've talked more about parenting than our own relationship. It seems like that is the more significant bond.

"Financially, I would be fine even if he wasn't in the picture. I have a job. I can afford to have a kid. I'm not dependent on someone else. I did feel dependent on him when I first found out, but as it's progressed, I don't really anymore. It was just a weird hormonal thing. I have plenty of girlfriends who have done IVF, two of them are single, one just had twins on her own by choice. Another big factor, just going ahead with this pregnancy, I really thought Ken was such a nice guy that even if things didn't work out between us, it would still be very civil. He trades dogs back and forth with his ex. One of the reasons they broke up is he wanted children and she didn't.

"The pregnancy has been unbelievably easy. My blood pressure is good, no gestational diabetes. I had an amnio, of course, because of our ages, and that was fine. I felt icky for three or four weeks, but I never even threw up. Everything has been so easy. I guess my body just didn't want to have children with the wrong man. Not that I think people's infertility is caused by their own situation. I have a lot of sympathy for people going through that. But in my case, especially since there was no concrete diagnosis all those years about why I wasn't getting pregnant, it really seems to be true that this child was waiting for the right daddy. Either that or Ken's got miraculous sperm."

While Leslie began trying to get pregnant when she was well within a typical woman's fertile years, many Gen Xers have delayed childbearing as they try to gain financial traction. This has led to a drop in fertility as women either are unable to conceive or simply don't have enough time left to have more than one child. As a result, the fertility industry has exploded. In 1992 there were just 1,802 attempts by women to become pregnant using donor eggs; by 2004 there were 15,175 attempts that produced 5,449 babies. Using donor eggs is now the fastest-growing infertility treatment.[2] And more women are becoming "mothers by choice" later in life after having invested heavily in the development of their careers.[3] Declining fertility and an increase in single-parent households have contributed to the shrinking size of the average American household, which dropped from 3.4 people to 2.6 people between 1960 and 2005, according to the U.S. Census Bureau.

And yet, for Generation X there's a countervailing trend that defies the overall statistics. Educated women in their thirties who earn a decent living not only are far more likely to get and stay married, they are also having more children than the average. The rate of both Hispanic and non-Hispanic white women of childbearing age giving birth to three or more children rose by 7 percent in the late 1990s (during the economic boom). The economic downturn after the dot-com bubble burst slowed the rate of third births, but it still remains above the average for baby-boomer women, largely because female managers and professionals are having more children. In 2002 professional women had double the number of children under eighteen at home as did women in similar positions in 1977, and women with a four-year college degree or more had triple the average number as did women with similar educational backgrounds in 1977.[4]

How these stats square with declining fertility and shrinking families is explained by the bifurcation of the middle class just as Gen X became the middle demographic of the middle class. According to *The Great Risk Shift* by Yale sociologist

Jacob Hacker, married couples with children today are twice as likely to file bankruptcy than married couples without kids. Families with kids have more than three times as much debt as married couples without kids, and nine times as much debt as single people. The gap in wealth between young and old families has grown enormously. In 1984 median household wealth of older families (parents between fifty-five and sixty-four) was four and a half times the median for families headed by twenty-five- to thirty-four-year-olds. By 2003 this median household wealth was nearly thirteen and a half times as great in older families. Contrary to convention wisdom, rising debt and falling wealth are not the result of increased consumer spending. According to Hacker, young parents in the 1990s spent less than their baby-boomer counterparts did in the 1970s. People with children today are 50 percent more likely than people without children to say they could get by no more than a week if the family suffered a financial hardship like job loss.[5]

Although there are few hard data to support the following theory, an educated guess as to why some women are increasingly ambivalent about having children is that struggling Gen Xers—whether they are creative types like MaryAnn Johanson and Jen Bekman or are simply having a hard time getting traction—are weighing the expense and hardship of raising kids and, therefore, opting to have only one or none at all. But Gen Xers who have stable financial lives and don't have fertility problems, such as Grant and Amy, are having more children and are as devoted as ever to raising a family even while maintaining careers. Despite having jobs, women spend about the same amount of time with their kids as women did in the

1960s, while fathers spend upwards of a third more of their time with kids than men in previous generations did.[6]

In fact, the most significant shift for post-boomer men is an unprecedented level of involvement with their kids, as a spate of recently published books can attest: *Alternadad* by Neal Pollack; *Pop Culture: The Sane Man's Guide to the Insane World of New Fatherhood* by Christopher Healy; *Daddy Needs a Drink: An Irreverent Look at Parenting from a Dad Who Truly Loves His Kids—Even When They're Driving Him Nuts* by Robert Wilder; *Crouching Father, Hidden Toddler: A Zen Guide for New Dads* by C. W. Nevius and Beegee Tolpa; *Keeping the Baby Alive till Your Wife Gets Home* by Walter Roark; *Mack Daddy: Mastering Fatherhood Without Losing Your Style, Your Cool, or Your Mind* by Larry Bleidner; *Bringing Up Baby: The Modern Man's Guide to Fatherhood* by Sam Martin; *The Guy's Guide to Surviving Toddlers, Tantrums, and Separation Anxiety (Yours, Not Your Kid's!)* by Michael Crider; and, my favorite of the bunch, *Punk Rock Dad: No Rules, Just Real Life* by Jim Lindberg, lead singer of the Warped Tour band Pennywise.

Although women still do more of the household chores and spend more time with their kids than men do, Generation X has closed that gap considerably, which is largely the result of increasingly flexible gender roles. Economists and co-authors Shelly Lundberg and Robert A. Pollak note that in advanced industrial economies where gender roles are inflexible, the rates of marriage and fertility among educated, professional women are significantly lower than among their counterparts in the United States. Without a *Sex and the City/Punk Rock Dad* breaking of the rules about who does the housework, changes the diapers, earns the money, and makes decisions about bedtime, etc., marriage and childbearing for educated, professional women are a much less desirable option.

The authors conclude: "As women's education levels and market wages have risen in Spain, Italy, and Japan, young men and women have been unable to commit to a non-traditional division of childrearing responsibilities and other household labor. In the absence of substantial changes in the norms governing marriage, marriage has become, at present, relatively unattractive to women in these countries." What's more—and again due to traditional social norms—those highly educated and successful women are not having children on their own either, thereby further dampening the fertility rate.[7]

This drop in fertility rates among educated, successful women outside of American culture is noted elsewhere. Yukako Kurose, a forty-five-year-old "career woman," told the *International Herald Tribune* that "Japanese work customs make it almost impossible for women to have both a family and a career."[8] One economic consequence of this is a much smaller workforce being burdened with supporting an aging population—a problem that the United States also faces, although less starkly.

Furthermore, although the Pew study on contemporary marriage and childrearing concludes that "in the United States today, marriage exerts less influence over how adults organize their lives and how children are born and raised than at any time in the nation's history," there is another side to the story for Generation X. On the one hand, conservatives have turned out to be correct that children raised in two-parent households do better educationally and by other outcome measures than single-parent households and stepparenting situations;[9] on the other hand, the alleged scourge of the American family and declining fertility has been misidentified as selfishness or a "lifestyle choice" by the Dan Quayles of the world. According to Lundberg and Pollak, improving financial and job security for young Americans would do more to foster marriage and childbearing than any other single factor.

What's more, the emergence of alternative parenting has actually bolstered fertility among gay couples and educated single professional women, such as Leslie, who—without her financial stability—might have elected to end her pregnancy, or mothers by choice who are actively seeking out single parenthood.

And ironically, it turns out Gen X's embrace of flexible gender roles has been the savior of a more traditional nuclear family configuration. Helped along by the bargaining power of financially independent women, Gen Xers' neo-traditional approach to domesticity has reestablished a commitment to marriage and childbearing—at least for one segment of the population—that approaches a rate not seen since the early 1960s.

11

Suburbia: A Tangent Universe

> "When they flood the house and they tear it to shreds, that destruction is a form of creation. . . . They just want to see what happens when they tear the world apart. They want to change things."
>
> —**Donnie Darko interpreting Graham Greene's short story "The Destructors" in his high school English class**

On the surface, Donnie Darko's white, upper-middle-class suburban teenage experience, circa 1988, looks pretty normal. He is cute and charming, with "intimidating" Iowa test scores. His parents are together and supportive. His older sister is on her way to Harvard; his younger tweenage sister is in a dance troop called Sparkle Motion. They live in a nice house in Middlesex, Virginia, where the worst things that kids do are smoking cigarettes and tormenting each other while waiting for the school bus in their neatly pressed school uniforms. But

Donnie Darko has emotional problems (which he announces cheerfully to the new girl while walking her home from school). He might even be psychotic. He sleepwalks and has an "imaginary friend" named Frank, a six-foot-tall, evil-looking rabbit who tells Donnie the world is going to end in twenty-eight days, six hours, forty-two minutes, and twelve seconds.

The 2001 Sundance hit and cult favorite *Donnie Darko* (played by then up-and-coming Jake Gyllenhaal) has been interpreted any number of ways—each debated endlessly, it seems, in some chat rooms. Of the most banal interpretations, it is a coming-of-age flick explained as a dream sequence and disguised as a psychological thriller. Another theory contends that no, Donnie Darko is not hallucinating. Rather, he is actually living in an inherently unstable Tangent Universe where the space-time continuum* has been disrupted; in this interpretation Donnie Darko's mission is to prevent the Tangent Universe from destroying the Primary one. First-time writer and director Richard Kelly (born 1975) has endorsed something closer to the latter theory: that it is really a sci-fi movie about the philosophy of time travel . . . *or is it?*

Donnie Darko lives in a Tangent Universe collapsing in on itself, alright—otherwise known as suburbia. For thousands of years, humans lived in close proximity to each other in walkable towns and cities, but that all changed when post–World War II suburbanization inexorably sprawled outward, chewing

*Space-time is a mathematical equation that combines space and time into a single formula called the space-time continuum. Space-time is usually interpreted as space being three-dimensional and time as the fourth dimension.

up the landscape and hastening, if not initiating, environmental destruction, social isolation, and class stratification. In just the past sixty years, development patterns have been radically altered from "walkable urbanism" to "drivable sub-urbanism," as described by Christopher B. Leinberger, a professor of real estate at the University of Michigan, Senior Fellow at the Brookings Institution, and author of *The Option of Urbanism*. Although there are examples of drivable sub-urbanism before the Depression and World War II slowed development, according to Leinberger that was "just a warm-up for the last half of the century, when drivable sub-urbanism became the basis of the American economy, the unofficial domestic policy, and the American Dream."[1]

But in a Tangent Universe, the American Dream is a nightmare.

It's all very deceptively beautiful and tranquil in suburbia, where nothing sinister exists in the immediate environment except (in the case of Donnie Darko) one's own dark thoughts. Toxic waste dumps; poor, starving children; third world slums; and dangerous minorities are nowhere in sight, while "emotionally disturbed" teenagers who question authority are treated behind closed doors with therapy and pharmaceuticals. Little wonder that Xers moved as far away as they could get—if not spatially, then psychologically—to Downtown, USA.

Previous generations of restless souls, rebels, bohemians, and draft dodgers moved west, overseas, back to the land, even to Canada. But for Generation X, milquetoast suburbia was conformist hell, a breeding ground for boredom, dysfunctional families, and emotional instability. "Real life" was lived in the city, where homeless crackheads and deinstitutionalized psychotics at least made things a little more interesting (and made one feel rather sane by comparison).

Welcome to the jungle.
It gets worse here every day.

The opening sequence of the video to "Welcome to the Jungle," Guns N' Roses' first hit from their 1987 album *Appetite for Destruction*, was filmed in La Brea, an area of Los Angeles that has since gentrified. Axl Rose steps off a bus dressed like a preppy, suitcase still in hand as he is tempted first by a drug dealer and then by a hot chick in fishnets. Guns N' Roses guitarist Slash, who is easily recognizable by his top hat and long black curly hair, is slumped in front of a cheap electronics store, clutching a bottle in a brown paper bag while TV screens flicker in the dingy window display (no architecturally cutting-edge Apple stores in this urban jungle). In the rest of the video, scenes of riot police and other urban ills are interspersed throughout a "live" performance of the song. At the end of the video, cut back to Rose, now fully decked out in hair-metal regalia, who is standing in front of the electronics store. He's watching the television screens, one of which shows images of his former preppy self in a straightjacket and electroshock headgear, screaming to break free.

Richard Kelly might think he made a sci-fi movie about time travel, but what he really made was a Gen X critique of suburbia—one much more sophisticated than the Guns N' Roses video. In one of the first scenes, Donnie Darko is giving his spot-on interpretation of "The Destructors," by Graham Greene, which takes place in 1950s London. In this short story, a group of disaffected but relatively harmless kids hang out in an empty lot and call themselves the Wormsley Common Gang, named after the area of London where they live. (Were this story set in America, the empty lot would have been the result of white flight, but in London it sits empty ten years after the Blitz of World War II.) The gang's new leader is Trevor (called T because Trevor is too much of an elitist name), whose anger and destructive tendencies are explained by the slippage of his upper-middle-class family. His father, formerly an architect but now a clerk, had "come down in the world," while his mother annoys the neighbors by "putting on airs" that she can no longer legitimately claim. T's "odd quality of danger, of the unpredictable" pushes the boundaries of the gang's juvenile delinquency; he convinces the heretofore innocuous kids to dismantle the last remaining house on Wormsley Common. Without the other houses, there really is no "common," and the beautiful 200-year-old house stands alone in a kind of suburban-like isolation before the gang destroys it and all of its bourgeois accoutrements:

> The kitchen was a shambles of broken glass and china. The dining-room was stripped of parquet, the skirting was up, the door had been taken off its hinges, and the destroyers had moved up a floor. Streaks of light came in through the

> closed shutters where they worked with the seriousness of creators—and destruction after all is a form of creation.[2]

Taken from the story, one of Donnie Darko's acts of destruction (as ordered by Frank the evil bunny) is to burn down a suburban mansion. The house is owned by Jim Cunningham, a local celebrity played by Patrick Swayze, who has gotten rich by peddling an absurd self-help formula in which life is represented by a single axis with fear on one end and love on the other. But when Donnie Darko burns down Cunningham's house, a kiddie-porn dungeon is revealed, exposing Cunningham as a fraud and, by extension, tearing off the façade of suburban utopia.

Thanks in part to Generation X, the disruption of the space-time continuum is being repaired, and people are now going back to the future—the future of walkable urbanism. (Although it is still just a trickle compared to suburban sprawl.) According to Leinberger, a resurgence of demand for walkable urbanism has taken place since the early 1990s, and "[t]his is in large part due to the resurgence of market demand for walkable urbanism since the early to mid-1990s."[3] Generation X moved from their suburban childhood homes to walkable towns and cities first for college and then for jobs, but also in search of a richer cultural experience—and then vowed to stay.

Elizabeth Kooy grew up in Hastings, Nebraska, a small historic town that might be called an example of "old urbanism." Life in this classic railroad community centered on its main street, with stores at the street level, apartments above, and homes that were mostly within walking distance but at most a carriage ride away. This model is now being re-created in far-flung suburbs and repackaged as "new urbanism," which in all but a few cases is simply gussied-up suburbanism without reliable public transportation or much diversity—either racial or economic. Because the overwhelming majority of residential housing has been built in the suburbs for fifty years, for people like Liz and her young family, until very recently the traditional suburbs would have been considered their only option. Not anymore. Liz and her husband, Adrian Codel, bought a house in the West Loop, a once heavily industrial area of Chicago, where they are now raising their two sons, Zane and Cael. It may look like an entirely different world from where she grew up, but in function, it has more in common with Hastings than with far-flung suburbia.* People live in close proximity to each other, shopping is within walking distance, and there is a mix of uses on most blocks.

"I can't stand the suburban thing," Kooy said, "where you drive from one parking lot to another. Part of it is an environmental concern, but it's just annoying to have to get in the car and drive and not have the opportunity to bike or walk or take public transportation. I read *Last Child in the Woods* when I had my first son. The book is about how people don't go outside

*Hastings's big claim to fame is the birthplace of Kool-Aid, invented by Edwin Perkins, who developed a process in 1927 for extracting the liquid from a popular drink called Fruit Smack, making it much cheaper to distribute. According to the Hastings Museum, during the Great Depression, Perkins cut the price of Kool-Aid in half to just 5 cents a packet. Young entrepreneurs sprung up across the country setting up Kool-Aid stands, helping to make Kool-Aid wildly popular. Coincidentally, he moved his entire operation to Chicago, not far from where Liz now lives.

anymore, about how kids in the suburbs have lost their connection with nature. There's no sidewalks. The lawns are all manicured. They're too overscheduled to even play in their own backyards. When I grew up, I could ride my bike a mile away and be in the country. We would play and make up stories. Now kids spend all their time in front of video games.

"We traveled all throughout my childhood to cities like Los Angeles and New York, but the pivotal moment was when I came to Chicago to get a master's in social work at the University of Chicago. I realized how much more there is to do in a city. I made a conscious decision not to move out to the suburbs. That will never be my plan. I fell in love with Chicago and never want to leave.

"When we looked into buying a place, it was tough to find something we could afford. But when we drove up to look at this area, I said, 'There's our house.' It's funny because there were trucks everywhere, all this activity on the street because of Fulton Market, with a lot of meatpacking storage units and fruit and egg places. It's busy during the day and there are only a few houses. This is an area where people never used to venture to. They even took out the El stop on the Green Line. They're talking about putting it back in now. It was just interesting to me, and it was in our price range, and close to downtown.

"We have lots of friends who moved out to the suburbs when they had kids, but they moved back to the city. They said the schools are great out there, but they realized with commuting, they're never around their kids. On the weekends they had to institute a rule to never leave the house unless they all went out together because otherwise they would never see each other. I work at home doing research and policy work for a nonprofit juvenile justice organization, and I have someone come in part of the day to help with childcare while I get some work done. My husband is a dentist and gets to work in fifteen minutes, sometimes he bikes or takes public transportation, and sometimes he drives. It depends on what else we have going on that day. But we have time to be a real family life here.

"When we bought the house, we knew we were going to have kids, but we didn't have them yet. We looked into the school thing, but we didn't want to get too paranoid about it. The parents' group that I go to drives me crazy, how people are worried about schools before the kid is even out of the womb. If you're going to live downtown and go to a private school, you have to have money. For us, there are plenty of decent public schools. You have to look and work at it, but it's not like you have to send them to a private school or they will not succeed in life, that they're doomed to failure. That's just not true. A lot of parents are getting together and making sure their community school is a good one. For me, I want my kids to have diversity, and I don't see that in the suburbs."

As noted by Liz, finding affordable housing in many of America's major cities has become increasingly difficult, a situation that would have been unimaginable even a decade ago. Increasing demand for walkable urbanism has led to a 40 to 200 percent price premium on urban housing compared to suburban housing. And this price premium is likely to increase as the housing bubble bursts; anecdotal evidence indicates that it is the single-family housing market in exurbia that is experiencing the worst price depreciations.[4]

But the Xer rejection of the way that suburbia has been built is more than simply a dislike of the isolation created by low-density land use and dependence on cars. Rather, it is the housing itself, a model that goes back to the first era of Creative Destruction, when industrialization in the nineteenth century made cities practically unlivable. In his 1991 book, *The Conscience of the Eye: The Design and Social Life of Cities,* Richard Sennett, a professor at both the London School of Economics and New York University, wrote: "The public world of the street was harsh, crime ridden, cold, and above all, confused in its very complexity." He went on to state that "the private realm sought order and clarity through applying the division of labor to the emotional realm of the family, partitioning its experience into rooms." Sennett noted that communal areas of the home gave way to activity-specific, divided rooms, with the man in the study, the woman in the kitchen, the children in their own separate bedrooms or play areas: "Separation created isolation in the family as much as it did on the street. . . . The hearth was supposed to give warmth, yet the division of labor [inside the house] gradually cast its own chill."[5]

Today's McMansion is essentially the same isolating nineteenth-century house on steroids, and, despite a growing preference among Generation X for better, more efficient design, the housing bubble in the first half of the decade only made matters worse. Like a supernova that burns brightest just before collapsing in on itself, McMansion developers went on their final building spree even after a book titled *The Not So*

Big House: A Blueprint for the Way We Really Live became an unlikely bestseller in 1998, garnering critical acclaim for the author, Sarah Susanka, a Minneapolis-based architect.[6] She was at the precipice of a "generational shift," according to market research conducted by Reach Advisors, a Boston-based marketing firm. Even Xers who prefer single-family houses want smaller homes built closer together with amenities that foster interaction with their neighbors, such as dog parks and walking trails. Ever the practical generation, wealthy Xers, too, prefer quality over quantity, and are less concerned than older generations with what a house says about one's status. They also would rather their private space foster family interaction than be divided into separate activity rooms. For decades, progressive urban planners have advocated for cities to promote mixed-use buildings and blocks, but the same could be said for a suburban house. Multi-use spaces are where families interact, and that interaction makes the difference between a home that is merely occupied and one that is truly lived in.

But rather than scale down to a more efficient design, McMansion builders just kept adding on to the already bloated floor plans. Media rooms, home offices, and hearth rooms—a poor imitation of a loft-like space, where the kitchen flows into eating and sitting areas anchored by a fireplace, while the formal living and dining rooms go unused—grossly expanded square footage,* despite a growing preference for something different.

---

*According to Census data published by the *Wall Street Journal* (September 12, 2007), median square feet of floor areas for new privately owned, single-family homes jumped from 1,560 in 1974 to 2,248 in 2006. The typical McMansion is 3,000 square feet or bigger.

One executive in the homebuilding industry told the *New York Times* in 2006: "We haven't been as quick to adapt to the market as we should have been." Why? "Most home builders are reluctant to change the formula that made them so profitable over the past 10 years," explained James Chung, president of Reach Advisors.[7]

The unsustainability of this Tangent Universe—where suburbia spreads unimpeded, families are isolated from their communities as well as each other, and environmental destruction is outsourced—didn't come into full consciousness until the housing bubble began to burst in 2006. What we as a society failed to contain is being corrected harshly by the market. The immediate ramifications are of course a record drop in housing prices and an unprecedented number of foreclosures—a catastrophe that, at the time of this book's publication, is still unfolding.* When all is said and done, 2 million people could lose their homes.[8] Meanwhile, due to changing housing preferences and demographics (only about a quarter of the population lives in a traditional family configuration), coupled with the housing crash and rising cost of gas, it is estimated that 40 percent of all large-lot, single-family houses existing in 2000 will be hard-pressed to find buyers by 2025.[9] And this is to say nothing of the real estate crash's effect on the overall economy. (That's a whole other book that has yet to be written.)

*According to the *New York Times*, economists at Goldman Sachs have predicted home prices will drop by 15 percent, or $3 trillion. Other forecasters have said the decline could be 20 percent or more. ("Reports Suggest Broader Losses from Mortgages," October 25, 2007.)

Regardless of the real estate crash, the long-term problems of energy use and global warming are only just beginning to be felt. Land development between 1950 and 1990 grew by 245 percent—or 2.65 times the population growth rate. In Atlanta over the same period, the population grew threefold while the developed landmass increased tenfold.[10] At the time this book was being written, the entire American Southeast was in the worst drought of its history, and Atlanta was just a few months away from being completely out of water—a situation that is exacerbated by inefficient land use (to name just one of any number of horrifying environmental stories that have come to dominate the news). Sprawl, of course, also means longer and more frequent car trips: today more than two-thirds of U.S. oil consumption is for transportation. Meanwhile, as of August 2007, $1.3 trillion has been spent on the war in Iraq.[11] This is almost the total amount that the American Society of Civil Engineers estimated in 2005 was needed over the next five years to minimally improve current infrastructure to prevent bridges from collapsing, as one did in downtown Minneapolis. (Thirteen people were killed in August 2007 when a major span fell into the Mississippi River during rush hour.)[12] Fixing America's infrastructure will be enormously expensive, but as Congressman Barney Frank said, we couldn't afford the Iraq War on September 10, 2001, either.

The effects of the most catastrophic real estate bubble in American history are still unfolding as of this writing, but for Generation X, once again, it's a mixed bag. For many people in this demographic, particularly people living in urban areas, housing simply became too expensive to purchase at all. For those who were able to enter the market, Xers were more likely to be first-time home buyers when prices were at their peak. What's more, although scant data exist, an educated guess is that this demographic is more likely to have engaged in risky financing, such as interest-only and adjustable-rate mortgages, increasing the likelihood of foreclosure. But people who bought early enough in gentrifying urban neighborhoods in most cities in the United States have unquestionably made a smart purchase that will, in all but the worst circumstances, increase their wealth even after the housing bubble completely deflates.

More importantly, Xers will continue to alter the course of development by demanding more efficient, better-quality design, be it in the suburbs or in cities. And by breathing new life into cities across the United States, the conservation movement evolved from "Birkenstock architecture"—homes made of straw bales built in the New Mexico desert—to "sustainability," spurring the whole green building movement, which is unquestionably linked to the resurgence of urbanism. Indeed, urbanism as a concept—in which cities are no longer thought of as outside of or disconnected from nature, but rather living-breathing organisms—has become surprisingly mainstream, and is the predominant philosophy driving the next generation of architects and designers, who are upending the old order not a moment too soon.

The reigning generation of "starchitects" is represented by Frank Gehry, whose twisted stainless-steel buildings are self-consciously out of context (not necessarily a bad thing), but are often incompatible with the environment. The roof of Gehry's concert hall in Los Angeles had to be altered when it was discovered that the intense LA sun, reflected by the shiny stainless steel, was creating hot spots, like a child using a magnifying glass to fry ants. Another stainless-steel roof on a Gehry building in Cleveland slopes in certain spots at such acute angles that dangerous chunks of snow and ice have slid off, conking people on the head. Gehry's generation of deconstructivist architecture cast aside the modernist "machine for living" approach to the built environment, which yielded some beautiful designs such as Philip Johnson's Glass House, but nonetheless often treated the humans inhabiting these buildings as dirty dishes to be stacked in the dishwasher for a proper cleaning. Neither camp paid much attention to human-centered design nor built with sensitivity to the surrounding environment.

The next generation of architects, however, is best represented by the husband-and-wife team Alejandro Zaera-Polo (b. Spain 1963) and Farshid Moussavi (b. Iran 1965), founders of Foreign Office Architects (FOA), who met at the Harvard Graduate School of Design. They reject flashy gestures that get repeated all over the world until any ten-year-old child can spot a Gehry building. "We love Gehry," Moussavi told a publication of the British Design Museum, "but our generation can't operate in the same way." Zaera-Polo, who used numerous ecological metaphors to explain their philosophy, including how the same grape varietal grown in Napa Valley will exhibit different characteristics than one grown in Chile, states, "Each building is like a species grown for a specific ecosystem, an antidote to homogenizing globalization," and "[w]e try to let the building grow by itself."[13]

It remains to be seen whether or not a pragmatic design aesthetic, the burgeoning ecological approach to the built environment, and the revitalization of cities will prevent the Tangent Universe of suburban sprawl from destroying the Primary one of walkable urbanism that has existed on earth for thousands of years. The fact is that none of these ideas are very new or revolutionary. Building on centuries of Western thought, landscape architect Ian McHarg articulated a theory in 1968 that he later called "creative fitting" to describe how humans adapt to nature and vice versa: "We need a general theory that encompasses physical, biological and cultural evolution . . . which includes criteria of creativity and destruction."[14]

12

"It's the End of the World as We Know It, and I Feel Fine . . ."

(Sandeep Kaushik, from flannel-shirted teenage stoner to reasonably responsible husband and father, as told to the author.)

There is a category of mental illness that will be in the DSM,* Delayed Onset Adulthood Syndrome. It's not unique to me. There are a lot of people that have gone through the same thing. Now I think, "Shit, I'm forty-one years old, house in Seattle, and a wife, two kids. What the hell happened?" I could break it down, but ultimately at some point you grow up even if you don't exactly feel or look grown-up. I just picked a harder pathway to get here.

I caught the tail end of the counterculture. For me, being an Indian kid in northern Virginia, I didn't have a grip on American culture. I finally found my way into American culture in

*The Diagnostic and Statistical Manual of Mental Disorders (DSM) is a handbook for mental health professionals that lists different categories of mental disorders and the criteria for diagnosing them.

FACTS:

Men who were in their thirties in 1974 had median incomes of about $40,000, while men of the same age in 2004 had median incomes of about $35,000 (adjusted for inflation).[1]

Only the top 10 percent of wage earners increased their income as much as the overall growth of U.S. productivity between 1966 and 2001.[2]

In 2007 the second richest man in America, Warren Buffett, took a survey of his office staff at Berkshire Hathaway and found that while he was paying 17.7 percent payroll and income tax, the average worker in the office paid 32.9 percent. He commented that "there wasn't anyone in the office, from the receptionist up, who paid as low a tax rate and I have no tax planning; I don't have an accountant or use tax shelters. I just follow what the US Congress tells me to do."[3]

my early to mid-teens through smoking pot, being a stoner, being the guy who was getting into trouble. That offered a whole way of looking at the world. You put on a flannel shirt, and people know exactly who you are. You're the smart, stoner guy. It's a type. I could fit in that way.

The other thing that really shaped my life, I lived "Morning in America." I spent my whole life watching the values I believe in lose over and over again, this continuous downward decline. I did phone-banking volunteer work for the Mondale campaign in 1984, and got totally turned off by it. It was disastrous. It was the worst campaign ever—until the next Democratic campaign. So I stopped voting. I thought Dukakis was a loser. I didn't vote again until 2004.

I went to Reed College [in Oregon], where I put some intellectual trappings onto this bohemian worldview; it was the antithesis of bourgeois existence. It was all about an experiential existence—traveling places, living in different cities, smoking and drinking in cafés, nailing two chicks at once. You haven't lived unless you've done these things.

I thought me and my friends, we were really special. We were touched by the gods. We were so clever and talented. In this effortless way, we were going to live the life without having to lift a finger. We were going to hang out on the porch, drink beer, and be incredibly successful. I was sure of it. It was a given. There was no thought about how to map this out. I just assumed, being who we were, having whatever skills or talents we had would take us there. I didn't realize smart people are actually a dime a dozen. A lot of people have talents. But do you know how to develop a career? Do you know how to make your way in the world?

It was a hard transition coming out of Reed College into the world. I got into trouble. It's all insipid and banal in some ways because it's all too common. But on a personal level, it has a lot of meaning in terms of shaping who I am. So I'm doing drugs and going nowhere and I decided I couldn't stay in Portland. I was the manager of a movie theater: running this cooperative movie theater and making like $6 an hour. So I moved to New York and got a job writing for a trade newspaper on Wall Street. I started at $16,800 a year; eventually I got a raise, so I think I made $17,200. I lived on Avenue B in 1989. One of our

Private-equity fund managers earn much of their compensation by taking a cut of clients' earnings, which is taxed at 15 percent instead of the 35 percent income tax rate that most wealthy earners pay. About 20 percent of hedge fund compensation is also taxed at 15 percent, a rate lower than most administrative assistants pay.[4]

Total public debt (government and individual), according to the U.S. Department of Treasury, is $9.1 trillion as of November 2007.

About 25 percent of U.S. government debt is held by foreign governments: Japan ($610.9 billion), China ($407.8 billion), the U.K. ($210.1 billion), and Middle Eastern oil-exporting countries ($123.8 billion).[5]

The U.S. government projects that at least thirty-six states will face water shortages within five years because of a combination of rising temperatures, drought, population growth, urban sprawl, and waste. The United States used more than 148 trillion gallons of water in 2000, according to the latest figures available as of November 2007, which is almost 500,000 gallons per person. The Intergovernmental Panel on Climate Change, a United Nations network of scientists, said this year that, by 2050, up to 2 billion people worldwide could be facing major water shortages.[6] New York City alone throws 1.4 billion gallons of treated wastewater into its rivers each day, which could be recycled and used as "gray water," i.e. for uses other than drinking.[7]

By the year 2050, the human population is projected to increase by about 3 billion, requiring an additional landmass the size of Brazil to grow enough food to feed everyone. More than 80 percent of the land that is suitable for raising crops is already in use.[8]

neighbors got gunned down in the doorway. I got robbed at gunpoint in Tompkin Square Park. Then it started to gentrify, so we moved out of the East Village to Williamsburg, near the bridge. It was really burned-out. But again, you could kinda tell it was going to change. But there were still drugs on every block. So I'm writing a column about the chemical market for the Wall Street trade paper. This is not what I thought I was going to do with my life.

So I decide to apply to grad school for the worst possible reasons, because I *could* and it would satisfy my parents. I got into Princeton. I thought it was going to be like my undergrad experience and I could put off having a nine-to-five job. I found out later that I was the last person they admitted, the lowest ranked. I met some interesting, smart people. But they were very careerist and took themselves seriously in a way that I never did. I did that for way too long. I got an MA in 1993 and I thought I should leave then but I didn't have a plan B. I didn't know what I wanted to do. So it was the path of least resistance to go for a PhD. I was sort of working on it and teaching. I spent a year in England and did all this research. I wrote a lot, some 300 pages. But six years later I still wasn't going to finish: I was going for a PhD in British history; my dissertation was going to be on ecclesiastical politics in the early seventeenth century. This was not a romp with two chicks.

I just hit the wall. What am I doing? I don't like teaching. I sucked at it. I hated it. I had been in this state of denial for five years. I was unhappy, but I had been unhappy for so long I didn't even notice it anymore. Liz, my future wife, was like, "Just bail. You don't want to do it." I realized I didn't know what I wanted to do but I had edited the Reed College paper, and I knew that I liked writing and journalism. I started freelance writing, which led to a full-time position [first at a weekly paper in Cleveland and then] in Seattle as a staff writer at *The Stranger*.

I started writing about politics on a lark. I heard about these Meet-Up things in March 2003. So I went to one here in Seattle expecting 15 people and there were 200 people 19 months before the presidential election. The place was packed for this obscure candidate. What the hell is going on? I wrote a 350-word piece about the

Trees are the most efficient way to remove carbon dioxide—responsible for global warming—from the atmosphere. The loss of primary forest since the year 2000, mostly to convert the land to agricultural uses, has been estimated at 6 million hectares annually, about six times the state of Connecticut.[9]

An international team of researchers has found that since the year 2000, the rate at which CO_2 has been pumped into the atmosphere is 35 percent greater than most climate change models have predicted. Alan Robock, associate director of the Center for Environmental Prediction at Rutgers University, said, "It turns out that global-warming critics were right when they said that global climate models did not do a good job at predicting climate change. But what has been wrong recently is that the climate is changing even faster than the models said. In fact, Arctic sea ice is melting much faster than any models predicted, and sea level is rising much faster than [Intergovernmental Panel on Climate Change] previously predicted."[10]

As of November 2007, the cost of the Iraq War will reach ten times its original projected cost of $50–60 billion, rising to $576 billion (which does not include hidden costs, which bring the price tag closer to $1.3 trillion), second only to World War II. It costs $200,000 a minute to keep troops deployed in Iraq.[11]

Between April 2003 and June 2004, $12 billion in U.S. currency was shipped from the Federal Reserve to Baghdad, in the form of forty *pallets of cash, weighing thirty tons,* where at least $9 billion has gone missing. The company that was hired to keep tabs on the outflow of money was a shell corporation; its address of record is a post office box in the Bahamas.[12]

Discretionary spending went up in George W. Bush's first term by 48.5 percent—not adjusted for inflation—which is more than double that under Bill Clinton in two full terms (21.6 percent). Defense spending under Bush has grown an average of 5.7 percent a year, compared to 4.9 percent a year under LBJ during Vietnam. Current annual defense spending—not counting war costs—is 25 percent above the height of the Reagan-era buildup.[13]

Meet-Up. I had only been in Seattle for a year, so I thought it was just a local thing. But my editor was like, "We need to cover this guy, Howard Dean." So *The Stranger* sent me to New Hampshire, and I wrote this profile of him that got a lot of circulation. Dean got Gen X culturally. We live in a Joe Millionaire culture, and the Democratic Party is babbling on about the decline of civility. Dean was nakedly partisan. That's what I found refreshing about it. I interviewed him in New Hampshire in May of '03. He was just rat-a-tat-tat. He was like a machine gun going off.

So I was writing about politics at *The Stranger*. I covered the Republican convention in New York, and the whole campaign, but I thought, where am I going next? I loved my job but I needed to make more money. We already had our first child and we were thinking about having another. At the time I wasn't at all wedded to Seattle, but I'm a pinball. I've always taken the path of least resistance. So I take a job doing political communications work. Since then I've been doing campaign consulting. I'm in the thick of it.

One of the things I like about Seattle so much: this place is where people like me can be in positions of relative power and authority, in charge behind the scenes, and having a significant impact. It never would have happened for someone like me in DC or New York. This is like candy-land for Gen X, a "creative class" sort of semi-utopia.

I'm not the kind of person that does a lot of mapping out of my future. I don't have a plan for life. I'm in this new phase of working on my own as a political/communications consultant, working for candidates and on ballot issues. I've carved out a niche for myself talking to the liberal media, doing new media outreach, so I know all the bloggers. You can do viral marketing through the blogs, but who knows what the future of that will be. I'm also a spokesperson for a congressional candidate. And on a contract basis, I'm doing public affairs and outreach for the private sector, which is a fancy way of saying I'm working for evil developers! Actually, they're the good guys, but not everyone sees it that way. It's all kind of piecemeal. Not only am I not the kind of person to plan for the future, but in my work you really *can't* plan for the future. I can't tell you what I'm doing next week.

As of November 2007, Bush had vetoed five bills, two for budgetary reasons: the State Children's Health Insurance Program (SCHIP) would have expanded health insurance for children in moderate-income families that earn too much to qualify for Medicaid but not enough to buy private insurance for their children (costing taxpayers an additional $35 billion over five years). Another veto, issued due to the bill's "excessive" costs (and the first to be overridden by Congress), authorized* $23 billion for water resource projects, including coastal restoration in Louisiana after Hurricane Katrina and improving the Florida Everglades.

Wall Street investment banks paid out a record $23.9 billion in bonuses in 2006; Goldman Sachs's CEO Lloyd Blankfein received $53.4 million, the largest ever granted to a Wall Street CEO.[14]

---

*Authorization bills don't actually allocate money; they simply lay out the priorities to be considered for funding. Appropriation bills specify what gets funded and by how much.

It's almost as if I don't have a future. You live in the present, and you go where the path of least resistance takes you.

For someone who had been completely turned off of politics, it's amazing that I like the political campaign world. Honestly, I'm interested in policy and government, but I'm more interested in winning and losing. How do you manipulate the power structure? How do you work the blogosphere? These things don't happen by magic. It's critical that people on my side know how to do it. The leaders of the netroots are all thirtysomething, Gen X types. They are very pragmatic about power. They're on the left, but they're not ideological.

I am fairly iconoclastic, with a kind of libertarian-liberal outlook. But I'm now learning how to become a team player. I'm going away from all my natural instincts and learning how to play well with others. It's a different way of thinking about the world. It means you play ball. My temptation was always to do the opposite, and I still get myself into trouble occasionally. In politics people don't like mavericks. In some sense I'm learning how to restructure my work life and how I exist in the world.

Due to the subprime mortgage fiasco, Wall Street investment banks have taken write-downs of $25 billion as of the third quarter of 2007, but that figure is projected to reach $64 billion when all is said and done.[15] Yet Wall Street firms were still expected to hand out another record $38 billion in bonuses at the end of 2007.[16]

Two million mortgage foreclosures are likely to occur by 2009 if home prices continue their downward spiral; $71 billion in housing wealth will be destroyed, an additional $32 billion would be lost because foreclosed homes tend to drive down the prices of other houses in the neighborhood, and states will lose $917 million in property tax revenue because of foreclosures.[17]

Personal bankruptcy rates increased by more than 60 percent between March 2006 and March 2007.[18]

It fits in with this Delayed Onset Adulthood Syndrome. Adults compromise with the world and work within the system. I'm forty-one years old and I'm just figuring this out now.

Until very recently, I thought I would have a job that paid the bills so I can lead my "real" life. I thought our lives were some kind of infinite performance art project. What's changed is that the countercultural stuff turned out to be a dead end. In Seattle I meet people all the time who remind me of myself, and I'm like, "Don't you guys realize this is not getting you anywhere—the lefty stuff?" If you want to get things done, you've got to understand the system and work to some extent in it and outside of it. You have to be sophisticated about power. The way things had been done, the way people on my side of the political divide were doing things was totally wrong. We were all so pure and politics is so dirty. And we wanted to be revolutionary and transformative but we don't want to mess with incremental change. I thought people who worked for incremental change were sellouts. I finally realized we didn't understand power; the Right understood what power was about. If you don't have

Seventy percent of the U.S. gross domestic product is based on consumer spending, financed by growing personal debt. As of August 2007, total U.S. household debt was $2.5 trillion, which is a 24 percent increase in the past five years. Total credit card debt was $915 billion. An estimated 43 percent of American households spend more than they earn each year.[19]

From 2004 through 2006, Americans took about $840 billion a year out of residential real estate—via sales, home equity lines of credit, and refinanced mortgages—using as much as $310 billion a year for personal consumption.[20]

Beginning in 2005 Americans have had a negative savings rate—the first time since the Great Depression.[21]

In 2007 Brazilian supermodel Gisele Bundchen began demanding to be paid in currencies other than the U.S. dollar, which, as of November 2007, had lost 34 percent of its value since 2001. She is one of "a growing list of rich people who have concluded that the currency can only depreciate because Americans led by President George W. Bush are living beyond their means."[22]

any power, you're just a bunch of losers in a bar talking out your asses about the world and not having any impact.

I always thought of myself as having one foot in adulthood and one foot in adolescence. I never thought I would end up so conventional, but I like what I do. I completely love Seattle. I go out drinking too much, but that's just because there's always someone to get a drink with. I've always been a restless sort, but I'm probably going to be here for the rest of my life and it doesn't seem that bad.

13

Convergence

Sometime in the fall of 2006, blobs of paint began appearing on street art around New York City, defacing not just indecipherable graffiti tags but clever social commentary. At first glance it seemed to be an act of mindless destruction, infuriating graffiti artists and connoisseurs of this increasingly mainstream form of expression (as one *New York* magazine writer put it, street art is graffiti with an MFA).[1] Even after it became clear there was a method behind the madness and the vandal was dubbed "the Splasher," people fulminated that there was nothing artistic about throwing splatters of cheap house paint on beloved street art (or worse: using a Super Soaker—Jackson Pollock would never have used a Super Soaker!). Who the Splasher is remains an open question,* but these acts of destruction (more than one hundred so far) were anything but

*The *New York Times* reported that one person was arrested but a couple of days later a small group of people crashed a street art event and distributed a sixteen-page tabloid titled "If We Did It This Is How It Would've Happened." As of this writing, the case was unresolved.

The ultimate in creative destruction: "The Splasher" purposely defaces street art by throwing paint on works by well-known graffiti artists and leaves notes calling them sellouts.

mindless. Usually accompanying the Splasher's handiwork were fliers with Nietzschean pronouncements about the Splasher's motives for destroying pieces by street artists who are selling out to the speculative and bubbly art market.

Not only have some big-name graffiti artists commanded serious dollars selling work in galleries and auction houses like Sotheby's, others such as Tats Cru (originally three South

Bronx natives who started out tagging subway trains back in the day) have long since gone commercial by simulating "graffiti" murals that advertise everything from Coca-Cola to Hummers (a shameless attempt to lend GM's "suburban assault vehicle" some street cred). In some cases, even the *pretense* of authenticity has been dropped by taking "graffiti" off the street and bringing it inside. A mural beneath teller windows in an East Village branch bank (a bank!) depicts a hot chick with pink hair, spray-painting a brick wall; one of her messages reads "Life is Love," accompanied by a heart (needless to say, North Fork Bank was probably not trying to make an ironic comment about Oprah-fied "street" art). It's not too much of a contradiction, then, to be saddened by the Splasher's acts of destruction while at the same time finding it hard to disagree with the critique, and yet also amused by the self-seriousness of the flier-manifestos, one of which concluded: "The passion for destruction is a creative passion. We are all capable of manifesting our desires directly, free of representation and commodification. We will continue manifesting ours by euthanizing your bourgeois fad."[2] Oooh. You go, girl.

Critics of the Splasher were particularly incensed by the spraying of a beloved Banksy piece in Williamsburg, Brooklyn. Perhaps the most successful street artist working today, Banksy has carefully protected and cultivated an anonymous persona while bombing major cities with politically provocative and often hilariously ironic social commentary. (One piece depicts a monkey and the words "Laugh now, but one day we'll be in charge.") He is believed to be Robert Banks,

Banksy—perhaps the most famous and highest-paid graffiti artist—satirizes gluttony in this London piece.

born in Bristol, England, in 1974, making him a youngish Gen Xer, but regardless of his identity or age, his sensibility is all irony all the time, espousing leftist politics while tweaking lefties at the same time. At a May Day demonstration in London, protest signs made by Banksy were handed out that read, "I don't believe in anything. I'm just here for the violence." He's also known for satirizing the art world by installing "fake" art in galleries and museums and seeing how long it takes for someone to discover it. At the British Museum in May 2005, Banksy mounted a piece of primitive "cave" art depicting a bison and a hunter, but instead of carrying a spear he's pushing a shopping cart. Accompanying the "pen-on-stone" drawing was a placard that clearly identified it as a hoax. The execution of the fake art and placard looked legit enough, however, that eight days went by before it was noticed. The piece is now in the museum's permanent collection.[3] Successful stunts like this over the years have considerably raised Banksy's bankability; one of his works fetched close to $600,000 at auction.[4]

"I have been called a sellout, but I give away thousands of paintings for free, how many more do you want?" Banksy wrote in an e-mail to *New Yorker* editor Lauren Collins for a profile she wrote about the artist. He goes on to state that "the money that my work fetches these days makes me a bit uncomfortable, but that's an easy problem to solve—you just stop whingeing [sic] and give it all away. I don't think it's possible to make art about world poverty and then trouser all the cash, that's an irony too far, even for me. I love the way capitalism finds a place—even for its enemies."[5]

This little story about a repeating cycle of graffiti that becomes respected street art that's then destroyed by more graffiti is the perfect metaphor for Creative Destruction, Joseph Schumpeter's economic theory. This story is particularly apt as the art form becomes increasingly entangled in supercapitalism's web (more on supercapitalism later). In his book *Capitalism, Socialism and Democracy*, first published in 1942, Schumpeter explained that the process of creative destruction "incessantly revolutionizes the economic structure *from within*, incessantly destroying the old one, incessantly creating a new one. This process of Creative Destruction is the essential fact about capitalism."[6]

In his definitive biography of Schumpeter, Thomas McCraw wrote:

> In his model [of creative destruction], recurring "Innovation" propels the economy, which exists in a state of constant tumult. "New Men" or "Entrepreneurs," operating within "New Firms," drive innovation. . . . Meanwhile, powerful elements of society resist major innovations, because they tend to wreak havoc on existing arrangements. As a result, "the history of capitalism is studded with violent bursts and catastrophes." It is no gentle process of adjustment but something "more like a series of explosions." [7]

McCraw goes on to explain that Schumpeter identified entrepreneurship with technological progress itself, but it is an asymmetrical process: "Innovating firms do not arise evenly throughout the economy. Instead, groups of these firms emerge just after an organizational or technological breakthrough."[8]

It's easy to see why Schumpeter has become all the rage in the era of Creative Destruction 2.0, as the technological revolution and globalization bring General Motors to its knees while catapulting Google, a search engine, ahead of GE and Coca-Cola.[9] *Business Week* featured Schumpeter in a December 2000 article titled "America's Hottest Economist Died 50 Years Ago."* In March 2002 *Wired* magazine ran an article about the increasingly celebrated economist titled "The Father of Creative

*Although Schumpeter was Austrian, he came to the United States to teach at Harvard in 1932, where he was in 1950, the year he died.

Destruction: Why Joseph Schumpeter Is Suddenly All the Rage in Washington." Despite his growing stature among the economic and political intelligentsia—and even within popular culture—it's probably safe to say that most Gen Xers have never heard of Schumpeter or the term "Creative Destruction." They're just living it.

Apryl Lundsten's career trajectory is the epitome of how the technological breakthroughs and innovations propelling Creative Destruction 2.0 have affected the everyday lives of a generation still grappling with having bridged the analog and digital worlds. Petite, blonde, and a multifaceted enthusiast—from architecture to pop culture to food and wine—Apryl is of course a free agent (as is her husband, David Spancer, who is in the television industry), who works out of an office in their mid-century modern house perched high in the hills of the still-gentrifying neighborhood known as Northeast Los Angeles.

"When I was in high school, I was taking a media production class, how to use cameras. I had it three periods a day because I loved being in there. My teacher really wanted me to learn how to use a computer. This was 1987. I really didn't want to learn how to use a computer; I figured I'm a writer, I'm going to use a typewriter. He forced me to learn. It was a RadioShack computer. Then my mom got a Mac at home about a year later. I became kind of addicted to it. The Mac was fun and the interface was easy, so I kept with that. I learned how to do graphic design. Then I was on the newspaper in high school and I would use the computer to do graphics and write. So technology had an impact even before I thought I was going to have a career using it.

"When I was in college—I was at film school at USC with an emphasis on screenwriting—the web was starting, so I was able to transfer my skills to web design. My first job after college was on campus, which also morphed into a web design thing. I had this film school background, so we worked with professors to do video and audio, which eventually became content for their websites. I was working on a freelance writing career outside of the day job, and all the stuff I learned from Real Audio transferred to radio production. So then I was freelancing for *Marketplace** and became a producer there for a year before going back to freelance. Then one day I was on Craigslist and came across a posting looking for someone who had radio experience to do a travel podcast about Santa Monica art and architecture.

"So I took that project on with a friend and afterwards she was like, 'Let's start a podcasting company.' I was so in my freelance mode, I didn't think I wanted to start a company. I don't know what my reluctance was. But she eventually convinced me. So we launched LA Pod Squad and the first thing we did was go after a marketing person from Anheuser-Busch who I had interviewed. He had been saying he wanted to revamp their marketing. My husband was like, 'Why would they even respond to you?' But they did respond to us right away and we got some meetings. It gave us the courage to go after anybody we found interesting.

"Until I had this podcasting production company, I didn't see how all these things fit together. In the 1990s there was this big thing, convergence: audio, video, web, etc. It was all going to be

**Marketplace* is a national business radio show produced for public radio.

one thing, but I didn't think I was going to experience my own convergence: writing, technology, and film production. I never would have seen that coming. It's finally starting to converge. It's ten years later and it's still not fully there. It could take another five or ten years, which is amazing. When I was first hearing about it, it was supposed to happen in, like, six months.

"I think back to high school, not wanting to learn how to use a computer because I thought there was nothing artistic about it. It's not that I thought it was a fad, but that it just wasn't for me. Frankly, I'm still not interested in technology. I'm interested in how it works for me, but I'm not reading *Wired* magazine. I use all these things very practically. I find that part of it exciting. It's amazing that all of these things that I did starting in high school led to where I am now."

Although this sounds like a nice and easy career trajectory, in fact Apryl and David have experienced pretty wild income swings—and this is to say nothing of their health insurance roller coaster: "My husband and I seem to switch health insurance every six months or so. If he gets a job that has insurance, we switch to that. Or if his Writer's Guild credits are up-to-date we use WGA insurance. But since his jobs only last a season—or pilots only a couple months at most—we are always changing insurance plans. David has decided he wants to get a 'real job' lately—because we want to have kids. Having both partners freelance terrifies us when it comes to having kids because there's no security. So we have definitely held off because of it and because of the ever-changing insurance. David is going to segue from being a writer to doing post-production work, hoping that it will be more steady."

As Apryl's story illustrates, the technological revolution has unleashed both creative and economic forces beyond anyone's imagination. To cite just one statistic: in April 1997 there were one million websites. By November 2006 there were 100 million.[10] Meanwhile, productivity, after stagnating for decades at 1.6 percent, took off in 1995, averaging 2.7 percent for ten years running.[11] Yet, in the time that Generation X has been the middle demographic of the middle class, globalization and technology created enough slack in the economy to cause people like Apryl and David to be jerked like bungee jumpers from low to high and back again. Whether or not the middle class will stop swinging wildly just short of hitting the ground or if there's in fact too much slack in the bungee cord remains an open question. So while Slackonomics has been creatively exhilarating, financially it has been very risky. (Even Alan Greenspan, steward of much of this riskiness as chairman of the Federal Reserve from 1987 to 2006, titled his memoir *The Age of Turbulence: Adventures in a New World.*)

"Indeed, the question of whether spreading globalization and information technology (IT) is strengthening or hollowing out our middle class may be the most paramount economic issue of our time," wrote Gene Sperling, economic advisor to President Bill Clinton, in a recent essay.[12] Not surprisingly, he makes the case that under Clinton, a rising tide lifted all boats, but under Bush it only lifted the yachts:

> As productivity grew 13 percent overall from 1995 to 2000, median family income kept up, growing 11 percent. From 1993 to 2000, every economic [group] saw income growth

> above 16 percent, with the strongest growth (23.4 percent) among the bottom 20 percent of earners. During the second half of this decade (2001 to 2006) . . . the story on shared prosperity could not have been more different. From 2000 to 2005, the typical working family saw its income fall 2.3 percent. And real wages actually fell for the first four years of the recovery.[13]

Narrowly focusing on one decade while favoring his former boss does not, however, answer the larger question of whether the middle class is being helped or hurt in the long run by globalization and the technological revolution. Sperling goes on to state that "it could take more than 50 years for labor costs in China and India—over 40 percent of the global labor market—to reach parity with those in the United States." And by reaching "parity," he politely means downward pressure on American middle-class wages. Sperling continues: "The result . . . is an increasing polarization of the workforce, with inequality rising more between the top 10 percent and the middle, rather than between the middle and the poorest."[14] By citing the relatively good times for middle- and low-income workers under Clinton, however, Sperling does put to rest one very important question that is endlessly debated between "individual responsibility" proponents and economic progressives: public policy does have an impact on people's everyday lives. Government cannot radically change the larger forces of globalization and technology, but clearly it can, at minimum, mitigate these forces on the margins—and perhaps even steer them in a particular direction. At no time in history has this been more critical.

The fate of the American middle class could very well be a stand-in for the future as a whole. This is truly a new era of Creative Destruction, not only altering everyday life for Generation X—from how we work, where we live, how we play, and when we marry and have children to our attitudes about love, humor, friendship, happiness, and personal fulfillment—but the world as we know it. Powerful forces have been unleashed in our lifetime, and to assume that it's all going to work out, that Creative Destruction will continuously renew the economy via radical transformation from within, could turn out to be the ultimate in naïveté.

Schumpeter argued strenuously in favor of capitalism at a time when socialism and communism were considered viable options ("the capitalist process, not by coincidence but by virtue of its mechanism, progressively raises the standard of life of the masses"). But he was also well aware of its shortcomings. Not only do people and industries get hurt in the churn, they become "free to make a mess of their lives" with enough "individualist rope" to hang themselves. What's more, capitalism sets up a tension "between two interests in society, the interest in present enjoyment, and the interest in the nation's economic future."[15] Schumpeter actually predicted that capitalism couldn't survive because governments would eventually quash creativity, an understandable conclusion when communism was a serious consideration. What Schumpeter didn't count on, however, is that capitalism can overwhelm democracy, and in the current age of Creative Destruction 2.0, it's working far too well.

Robert Reich, former labor secretary under Bill Clinton and professor of public policy at the University of California, Berkeley, argues in *Supercapitalism: The Transformation of Business, Democracy, and Everyday Life* that the latest technological revolution has mutated from democratic capitalism into supercapitalism. He states that

> the critical ingredient igniting globalization was a raft of new transportation and communications technologies, mostly associated with fighting the Cold War—cargo ships and cargo planes, overseas cables, steel containers and, eventually, satellites bouncing electric signals from one continent to another—that drastically reduced the cost of moving things from one point on the world's surface to another. . . . By the 1970s, gadgets dreamed up to improve military production were finding their ways into computerized machine tools, robots, and computer-aided design and manufacturing—all of which allowed things to be made at low unit cost. . . . New technologies had similar effects on services. Banking, insurance, and telecom could be customized to the needs of particular users. By the 1990s, the Internet also vastly increased the number of ways services could be distributed, including advertising and marketing directed to specific groups of people who shared special tastes or interests. Consumers had access to search engines and online reviews that matched them even more precisely with sellers who would give them exactly what they needed at the best price.[16]

All of this, Reich argues, turned out to be great for the individual as consumer and investor (to which I would add entrepreneur), but it has also resulted in the weakening of citizenship and democracy. This is essentially the problem Schumpeter meant when he said there was tension "between present enjoyment and the nation's economic future."[17] As the individual has triumphed over the collective, Generation X has adapted exceedingly well. But although the wisdom of crowds* may generate new innovations and creative solutions, it unfortunately does not provide the will or the mechanisms to implement policies that benefit the greater good at the expense of the individual. Mind-boggling income inequality, global warming, and the tragedy of the commons**—all of which are the result of capitalism in overdrive—do not get solved through individuals acting in their own best interest.

Not only have our weakened democratic institutions failed to keep supercapitalism in check, current economic models are no help, either. As evolutionary biologist Edward O. Wilson pointed out in his book *Consilience: The Unity of Knowledge,* economic models fall short because they are

> sealed off from the complexities of human behavior and the constraints imposed by the environment. As a result, economic theorists, despite the undoubted genius of many, have

---

**The Wisdom of Crowds: Why the Many Are Smarter Than the Few and How Collective Wisdom Shapes Business, Economies, Societies and Nations* is a book by James Surowiecki advancing a theory that aggregation of information in groups results in ideas, innovations, and decisions that are often better than could be produced by any single member of the group. (New York: Doubleday, 2004.)

**The tragedy of the commons is when public resources are not adequately protected and therefore tend to get exploited, such as overfishing the oceans.

> enjoyed few successes in predicting the economic future, and they have suffered many embarrassing failures. . . . [T]he theorists cannot answer definitively most of the key macroeconomic questions that concern society, including the optimal amount of fiscal regulation, future income distribution within and between nations, optimal population growth and distribution, long-term financial security of individual citizens, the roles of soil, water, biodiversity, and other exhaustible and diminishing resources, and the strength of "externalities" such as the deteriorating global environment. The world economy is a ship speeding through uncharted waters strewn with dangerous shoals. There is no general agreement on how it works.[18]

It could very well be up to Generation X to figure this out, to bring supercapitalism back into balance with an infusion of democracy and to start grappling with the limitations of what acting as individuals acting in their own self-interest can really do for the common good. As Reich points out, individual values and actions too often are divergent.[19] As consumers we demand the absolute lowest prices possible while amassing attics and garages full of crap we don't need, yet lament that Wal-Mart employees are underpaid and often lack health insurance. But just as Wal-Mart management is not inherently evil, neither is the average consumer inherently hypocritical or the average citizen inherently cynical and apathetic. Our democratic institutions and civil society have been weakened by supercapitalism—i.e., the takeover of politics and government by corporate interests—and people have adjusted accordingly.

It may take a global catastrophe—economic, environmental, or both—to alter this balance of power (and it should be noted that advocating for the weakening of corporate influence in the political realm is not the same as being anti-corporate—in fact, to the contrary). But when the circumstances become too dire to ignore, we will be forced to address the unsustainability of this imbalance, and people will be amazed at how quickly the will of the common good comes forcefully back into play. In other words, human nature is malleable. People did not suddenly become more conformist in the 1950s, more altruistic in the 1960s, crazier in the 1970s, greedier in the 1980s, more creative in the 1990s, or more corrupt in the 2000s. People adapt to the circumstances of the time. But these are extraordinary times that may very well require more than mere adaptation. We can now create and destroy on a global scale: by plundering the resources of the earth and its surrounding environs and irrevocably altering plant and animal life as we know it.

Generation X has long been known for eschewing politics and, in my estimation, for good reason. As the saying goes, refusal to participate is not the same thing as apathy. Right now the political process is pretty much bankrupt and ripe for some serious Creative Destruction, which, by definition, happens from within. But "within" does not mean it's going to start inside the Washington beltway. New infrastructure is being laid by Generation X far outside the realm of electoral politics and the corporate lobbying machine that corrupts it. An entrepreneurial spirit is being brought to the public realm through Internet organizing (as the Howard Dean campaign discovered), to social welfare through market-based philanthropy (such as the Acumen Fund), and to collective volunteerism through open-source activism (such as Architecture for Humanity). Whether or not one agrees with the politics of these organizations—or even knows what the hell they do—is beside the point. They represent creative new approaches to advancing the common good, normally the purview of government, which has all but abdicated its responsibility to anything other than greasing the skids for corporations to increase their profits.*

But let's be clear: signing a petition online or watching a debate on YouTube rather than old-fashioned TV does not fundamentally alter the equation. Internet organizing, open-source activism, and the like cannot replace government—even a grossly incompetent one, as has been demonstrated in New Orleans. Increasing the bandwidth of political engagement can, however, bring people back into the public realm, at which point change can finally happen from within. Indeed, the process of Creative Destruction doesn't renew capitalism by throwing it out as an economic system, and the same could be said for democracy. But we are in danger of losing it (and as we have seen in China, capitalism does not require democracy in order to function). Far too few Americans are even remotely engaged in the public marketplace where individual interests are reconciled with the common good, which are increasingly in conflict with each other. Actively engaging these conflicts

*Goldman Sachs found that more than 40 percent of its record growth in profits of the past five years was due to "the historically low share of national income going to labor," according to Sperling.

through democracy will not be fun—but it's not impossible and will most certainly be necessary. Yes, markets are self-correcting (even the public marketplace)—eventually. But how devastating the correction will have to be is, like it or not, up to us: a generation that started young adulthood as outliers and losers, but has since bridged the analog and digital worlds, created alternatives to Corporate America, endured the dot-com and real estate bubbles, adapted to and even pioneered the technological revolution and globalization without much in the way of security (i.e., universal health insurance, pensions, etc.), transformed long-standing institutions such as marriage and parenthood—and all the while maintaining our sense of humor. We're going to need it.

NOTES

Introduction: Bridging the Analog and Digital Generations

1. Patrick Reddy, "Generation X Reconsidered," *Buffalo News,* February 10, 2002.

2. "Campaigns Hunt Votes Among 'Anxious Xers,' 'Angry Independents,'" *Bloomberg News,* August 1, 2007.

1. My Future's So Bright, I Gotta Wear Shades

1. Richard Dawkins, *The Selfish Gene* (New York: Oxford University Press, 2006), 2.

2. Gregg Easterbrook, "The Real Truth About Money," *Time,* January 17, 2005, A32–A34.

3. Peter Cappelli, "The Impact of Managerial Layoffs, Wisdom from Wharton," *The Chief Executive,* June 1992.

4. Geoffrey T. Holtz, *Welcome to the Jungle* (New York: St. Martin's, 1995), 151.

5. Jeff Leeds, "We Hate the '80s," *New York Times,* February 13, 2005.

2. The Outliers

1. Douglas Coupland, *Generation X: Tales for an Accelerated Culture* (New York: St. Martin's, 1991), 139.

2. Coupland, 80, 54, 91.

3. http://en.wikipedia.org/wiki/Marshall_Mcluhan.

4. Marshall McLuhan, *Understanding Me* (Toronto: M & S, 2003), 3.

5. McLuhan, xxi.

6. Geoffrey T. Holtz, *Welcome to the Jungle: The Why Behind "Generation X"* (New York: St. Martin's Griffin, 1995), 160.

7. Daniel Gross, "Thy Neighbor's Stash," *New York Times Sunday Book Review*, August 5, 2007.

8. David Callahan, Tamara Drout, and Javier Silva, "Millions to the Middle: Three Strategies to Expand the Middle Class," Demos Think Tank (Report), August 30, 2004: 26.

9. "Life in the Bottom 80 Percent," editorial, September 1, 2005. *New York Times*,

10. Matt Miller, "How to Run a Budget Like an Idiot," CNN money.com and *Fortune*, June 11, 2007.

11. Anna Bernansek, "Income Inequality and Its Costs," *New York Times*, June 25, 2006.

3. Cunt

1. Daniel McGinn, "Marriage by the Numbers," *Newsweek*, June 5, 2006.

2. Catherine M. Orr, "Charting the Currents of the Third Wave," *Hypatia* 12, no. 3 (Summer 1997): 29–45.

3. *Time*, June 29, 1998.

4. Robert Longley, "Why Women Still Make Less Than Men," September 1, 2004. http://usgovinfo.about.com/cs/censusstatistic/a/womenspay.htm.

5. Robert Longley, "Gender Wave Gap Growing, Census Data Show," September 1, 2004. http://usgovinfo.about.com/od/censusandstatistics/a/paygapgrows.htm.

6. David Leonhardt, "Gender Pay Gap, Once Narrowing, Is Stuck in Place," *New York Times*, December 24, 2006.

7. J. D. Nordell, "Positions of Power: How Female Ambition Is Shaped," *Slate*, November 21, 2006. http://www.slate.com/id/2154331/?nav=tap3.

8. Daniel McGinn, "Twenty Years Later." http://www.msnbc.msn.com/id/12940306/site/newsweek.

4. I'm a Loser, Baby, So Why Don't You Pay Me

1. David G. Myers, *Intuition: Its Powers and Perils* (New Haven, CT: Yale University Press, 2002).

2. Jacob S. Hacker, *The Great Risk Shift* (New York: Oxford University Press, 2007), 31.

3. Thomas Frank, "Alternative to What?" *Baffler* 5 (1993); Frank and Weiland, 145–61.

4. John Leland, *Hip: The History* (New York: HarperCollins, 2004), 286.

5. Ibid., 306.

6. Hacker, 29.

7. Richard Miniter, "Generation X Does Business," *American Enterprise*, July/August 1997.

8. "Study: Free Agent Workforce Grows," *Business and Legal Reports*, February 11, 2003. http://hr.blr.com/news.aspx?id=8153.

9. Leland, 288.

6. Funny Weird or Funny Ha-Ha? . . . Hey, Why Limit Yourself!

1. Matt Sharkey, Keepgoing.org. http://www.keepgoing.org/issue20_giant/the_big_fish.html.

2. Ibid.

3. Joe Rhodes, "A Nerd Gone Wild Gives Voice to His Inner Rat," *New York Times*, June 24, 2007.

4. Peter Hyman, "Alt Comedy Goes Rock and Roll," *Spin* (January 2006): 75.

5. http://en.wikipedia.org/wiki/Arthur_Koestler.

6. Arthur Koestler, *The Act of Creation*, rep. ed. (London: Penguin, 1990). Emphasis in original.

7. Sandra Sugawara, "Americans Bank on Stock: Nearly 50 Percent of Households Put Faith in Market," *Washington Post* I, October 22, 1999.

8. Figures compiled for author by Heather Boushey of the Center for Economic and Policy Research.

9. Erica L. Groshen and Simon Potter, "Has Structural Change Contributed to a Jobless Recovery?" Federal Reserve Bank of New York annual report, vol. 9, no. 8 (August 2003). http://www.newyorkfed.org/research/current_issues/ci9-8/ci9-8.html.

10. Taken from a video of his talk, posted on the internet by Columbia Political Union, October 6, 2005.

11. Koestler.

7. Gonna Get Me Some Happy

1. http://culturalpolicy.uchicago.edu/conf1999/schamus.html.

2. Jennifer Senior, "Some Dark Thoughts on Happiness," *New York*, July 17, 2006.

3. Luigino Bruni and Pier Luigi Porta, eds., "Building a Better Theory of Well-Being," *Economics and Happiness: Framing the Analysis* (New York: Oxford University Press, 2006), 29–64.

4. Bruni and Porta, 25.

5. "Busters Have Work Ethic All Their Own," *USA Today*, July 20, 1993: B1; "GENERATION X: What They Want in Their Jobs and Careers," *Industry Week*, October 3, 1994: 19.

6. "No Place Like Home in Tomorrow's World," *The Independent* (London), June 10, 1998.

7. Anke Zimmermann and Richard A. Easterlin, "Happily Ever After? Cohabitation, Marriage, Divorce, and Happiness in Germany," *Population and Development Review* 32, no. 3 (2006): 511–528.

8. Sherry B. Ortner, "Generation X: Anthropology in a Media-Saturated World," *Cultural Anthropology* 13, no. 3: 414–440.

9. Pew Research Center for the People and the Press, "Americans See Less Progress on Their Ladder of Life," September 14, 2006.

10. Pew Research Center for the People and the Press, "Are We Happy Yet?," February 13, 2007.

11. Pew, "Americans See Less Progress. . . ."

12. Stefan Klein and Stephen Lehman, *The Science of Happiness: How Our Brains Make Us Happy—And What We Can Do to Get Happier* (New York: Marlowe & Company, 2006).

13. Donald A. Norman, *Emotional Design: Why We Love (or Hate) Everyday Things* (New York: Basic Books, 2005), 19.

8. Friends: The Newish New Thing

1. Ethan Watters, *Urban Tribes: A Generation Redefines Friendship, Family and Commitment* (New York: Bloomsbury, 2003).

2. Michael J. Weiss, "GREAT Expectations—Baby Boomer Wealth Forecasts Wilt," *American Demographics*, May 1, 2003.

3. http://www.sfgrotto.org/index.html.

4. Ibid.

5. Elizabeth Currid, *The Warhol Economy* (Princeton, NJ: Princeton University Press, 2007), 4.

6. John Seabrook, "Transplant," *The New Yorker*, June 11, 2007.

7. John Howkins, *The Creative Economy: How People Make Money from Ideas* (New York: Allen Lane, 2001); Richard Florida, *The Rise of the Creative Class* (New York: Basic Books, 2002).

8. Jim Black, "Gen Xers Return to College: Enrollment Strategies for a Maturing Population," American Association of Collegiate Registrars and Admissions Officers, trade organization article, Washington, DC, 2003.

9. Alison Stein Wellner, "The Mobility Myth," *Reason*, April 2006.

10. "Social Isolation in America: Changes in Core Discussion Networks over Two Decades," *American Sociological Review* 771 (June 2006): 353–75.

11. Ann Hulbert, "Confidant Crisis," *New York Times*, July 16, 2006.

12. Ibid.

13. Po Bronson and Ashley Merryman, "Has Being Married Gone out of Style?" *Time*, October 18, 2006.

14. Watters, 101.

15. Ibid.

9. Love: Is It Real or Is It Memorex?

1. http://www.reelviews.net/movies/w/waking_life.html.

2. Stephanie Coontz, *Marriage, a History: From Obedience to Intimacy, or How Love Conquered Marriage* (New York: Viking, 2005), 146.

3. The divorce rate more than doubled between 1966 and 1979. Ibid., 261.

4. Ibid., 308.

5. "The Science of Love: Love Is All About Chemistry," *The Economist*, February 12, 2004.

6. Helen Fisher, *Why We Love: The Nature and Chemistry of* Love, (New York: Henry Holt, 2004).

7. Edward O. Wilson, *Consilience: The Unity of Knowledge* (New York: Alfred A. Knopf, 1998), 231–32.

8. "The Science of Love," *The Economist*, February 12, 2004.

9. Sam Roberts, "The Shelf Life of Bliss," *New York Times*, July 1, 2007.

10. "The Science of Love."

11. Coontz, 260.

12. Sam Roberts, "51% of Women Are Now Living Without Spouse," *New York Times*, January 16, 2007.

13. Sam Roberts, "To Be Married Is to Be Outnumbered," *New York Times*, October 15, 2006.

14. Coontz, 268. Emphasis added.

15. Ibid.

16. Po Bronson, "Will This Marriage Last?" *Time*, June 30, 2006.

17. Coontz, 310.

10. The Breeders

1. Pew Research Center, "As Marriage and Parenthood Drift Apart, Public Is Concerned About Social Impact, July 1, 2007. http://pewresearch.org/pubs/526/marriage-parenthood.

2. Peggy Orenstein, "Your Gamete, Myself," *New York Times*, July 15, 2007.

3. Jennifer Egan, "Wanted: A Few Good Sperm," *New York Times Sunday*, March 19, 2006.

4. Haya El Nasser, "For More Parents, 3 Kids Are a Charm," *USA Today*, March 9, 2004. http://www.usatoday.com/news/nation/2004-03-09-cover-three-kids_x.htm.

5. Jacob Hacker, *The Great Risk Shift* (New York: Oxford University Press, 2006), 91, 94.

6. Ibid.

7. Shelly Lundberg and Robert A. Pollak, "The American Family and Family Economics," *Journal of Economic Perspectives* 21, no. 2 (Spring 2007): 3–26.

8. Martin Fackler, "Career Women in Japan Find Blocked Path," *International Herald Tribune*, August 5, 2007.

9. Lundberg and Pollak, 19.

11. Suburbia: A Tangent Universe

1. Christopher B. Leinberger, *The Option of Urbanism* (Washington, DC: Island Press, 2008), 5.

2. Graham Greene, *Twenty-one Stories* (New York: Penguin, 1991).

3. Leinberger, 15.

4. Leinberger, 99.

5. Richard Sennett, *The Conscience of the Eye: The Design and Social Life of Cities* (New York: W. W. Norton, 1990), 27–28.

6. Sarah Susanka, *The Not So Big House: A Blueprint for the Way We Really Live* (Newtown, CT: Taunton, 1998).

7. "Younger Buyers Want Better, Not Bigger," *New York Times*, May 7, 2006.

8. "Borrowers Face Dubious Charges in Foreclosures," *New York Times*, November 6, 2007.

9. Leinberger, 105.

10. Leinberger, 106.

11. "War at Any Price?" Report of the Congress Joint Economic Committee, November 2007.

12. http://www.asce.org/pressroom.

13. http://www.designmuseum.org/design/foreign-office-architects.

14. Ian McHarg, *To Heal the Earth: Selected Writings of Ian L. McHarg*, ed. Frederick Steiner (Washington, DC: Island Press, 1998), 7.

12. "It's the End of the World as We Know It, and I Feel Fine . . ."

1. Economic Mobility Project, May 25, 2007. www.economicmobility.org.

2. Jacob Hacker, *The Great Risk Shift* (New York: Oxford University Press, 2006), 64.

3. "'I Should Pay More Tax,' says U.S. Billionaire Warren Buffett," *The Guardian*, October 31, 2007. http://www.guardian.co.uk/business/2007/oct/31/usnews.

4. "Democrats Split over Bill Affecting Backers," *Washington Post*, November 7, 2007.

5. Ibid.

6. "Much of U.S. Could See a Water Shortage," Associated Press, October 26, 2007. http://ap.google.com/article/ALeqM5gsBhi0vfVCHrE0eSckT5ZnADWxwD8SH34A04.

7. Vertical Farm Project, http://verticalfarm.com.

8. Ibid.

9. United Nations Secretariat of the Convention on Biological Diversity, "Global Biodiversity Outlook 2," 2006. http://www.biodiv.org.

10. "Carbon Dioxide Levels Rising Much Faster Than Expected," Fox News, October 24, 2007, http://www.foxnews.com/story/0,2933,304272,00.html.

11. "CNN: Price of Iraq War 10 Times Pre-war Predictions," *The Raw Story*, November 2, 2007.

12. Donald L. Barlett and James B. Steele, "Billions over Baghdad," *Vanity Fair*, October 2007.

13. "Bush Is the Biggest Spender Since LBJ," *McClathy Newspapers*, October 24, 2007. http://www.mcclatchydc.com/227/story/20767.html.

14. "It's a Wall Street Bonus Bonanza," *USA Today*, December 20, 2006. http://www.usatoday.com/money/industries/brokerage/2006-12-20-wall-st-bonuses_x.htm.

15. "Wall Street's Subprime CDO Write-downs Seen $64 Billion," *Reuters*, November 8, 2007. http://www.reuters.com/article/ousiv/idUSN0823401520071108.

16. "Wall St. Handing Out Record Bonuses Despite Layoffs, Stock Market Woes," *New York Daily News*, November 20, 2007.

17. "Reports Suggest Broader Losses from Mortgages," *New York Times*, October 25, 2007. http://www.nytimes.com/2007/10/25/business/25mortgage.html.

18. Joseph E. Stiglitz, "The Economic Consequences of Mr. Bush," *Vanity Fair*, December 2007.

19. "The Catastrophist View," *New York* magazine, October 28, 2007. http://nymag.com/guides/money/2007/39952.

20. "Homeowners Feel the Pinch of Lost Equity," *New York Times*, November 8, 2007. http://www.nytimes.com/2007/11/08/business/08borrow.html?hp.

21. Bureau of Economic Analysis, Personal Income and Outlays, December 2006.

22. "Supermodel Bundchen Joins Hedge Funds Dumping Dollars," *Bloomberg News*, November 5, 2007. http://www.bloomberg.com/apps/news?pid=20601087&sid=aCs.keWwNdiY&refer=home.

13. Convergence

1. Sam Anderson, "The Vandalism Vandal," *New York* magazine, May 28, 2007.

2. "For Vandals, an Ironic Target: Street Artists," *New York Times*, January 28, 2007.

3. "Banksy: Wall and Piece," *Century*, 2006.

4. "Elusive Artist Banksy Sets Record Price," Reuters, London, April 25, 2007. http://uk.reuters.com/article/entertainmentNews/idUKL2531915420070425.

5. Lauren Collins, "Banksy Was Here: The Invisible Man of Graffiti Art," *The New Yorker*, May 14, 2007.

6. Joseph Schumpeter, *Capitalism, Socialism and Democracy* (New York: Harper & Brothers, 1942).

7. Thomas K. McCraw, *Prophet of Innovation: Joseph Schumpeter and Creative Destruction* (Cambridge, MA: Belknap Press, 2007), 254–55.

8. McCraw, 356.

9. "Google Surpasses Microsoft as World's Most-visited Site," *San Francisco Chronicle*, April 25, 2007. http://www.sfgate.com/cgi-bin/article.cgi?f=/c/a/2007/04/25/GOOGLE.TMP&type=business.

10. New Media Institute, http://www.newmedia.org/articles/35/1/There-are-Now-More-Than-100-Million-Web-Sites-on-the-Internet/Page1.html.

11. Gene Sperling, "Rising-Tide Economics," *Democracy: A Journal of Ideas*, no. 6 (Fall 2007).

12. Ibid.

13. Ibid.

14. Ibid.

15. McCraw, 351, 433.

16. Robert Reich, *Supercapitalism: The Transformation of Business, Democracy, and Everyday Life* (New York: Knopf, 2007), 64.

17. McCraw.

18. Wilson, 197–98.

19. Reich, 90.

BIBLIOGRAPHY

Anderson, Chris. 2006. *The Long Tail: Why the Future of Business Is Selling Less of More*. New York: Hyperion.

Baird, Jonathan. 1998. *Day Job: A Workplace Reader for the Restless Age*. Boston: Allen & Osborne.

Banksy. 2006. *Wall and Piece*. New York: Century.

Bruni, Luigino, and Pier Luigi Porta, eds. 2006. *Economics and Happiness: Framing the Analysis*. New York: Oxford University Press.

Coontz, Stephanie. 2005. *Marriage, a History: From Obedience to Intimacy, or How Love Conquered Marriage*. New York: Viking.

Coupland, Douglas. 1991. *Generation X: Tales for an Accelerated Culture*. New York: St. Martin's Press.

Currid, Elizabeth. 2007. *The Warhol Economy: How Fashion, Art and Music Drive New York City*. Princeton, NJ: Princeton University Press.

Ehrenreich, Barbara. 1989. *Fear of Falling: The Inner Life of the Middle Class*. New York: Knopf.

Faludi, Susan. 1991. *Backlash: The Undeclared War Against American Women*. New York: Crown.

Fisher, Helen. 2004. *Why We Love: The Nature and Chemistry of Romantic Love*. New York: Henry Holt.

Frank, Thomas, and Matt Weiland. 1997. *Commodify Your Dissent: Salvos from* The Baffler. New York: W. W. Norton.

Gilbert, Daniel. 2006. *Stumbling on Happiness*. New York: Knopf.

Greene, Graham. 1983. "The Destructors." *Twenty-One Stories*. New York: Penguin Books.

Greenspan, Alan. 2007. *The Age of Turbulence: Adventures in a New World*. London: Penguin.

Hacker, Jacob S. 2006. *The Great Risk Shift: The New Economic Security and the Decline of the American Dream*. New York: Oxford University Press.

Holtz, Geoffrey T. 1995. *Welcome to the Jungle: The Why Behind "Generation X."* New York: St. Martin's Press.

Klein, Stefan, and Stephen Lehmann. 2006. *The Science of Happiness: How Our Brains Make Us Happy*. Washington, DC: Marlowe & Company.

Koestler, Arthur. 1976. *The Act of Creation*. New York: Random House.

Le Corbusier. 1985. *Towards a New Architecture*. Mineola, NY: Dover.

Leinberger, Christopher B. 2007. *The Option of Urbanism: Investing in a New American Dream*. Washington, DC: Island Press.

Leland, John. 2004. *Hip: The History*. New York: HarperCollins.

Lethem, Jonathan. 1999. *Motherless Brooklyn*. New York: Doubleday.

Lowenstein, Roger. 2004. *Origins of the Crash: The Great Bubble and Its Undoing*. London: Penguin.

McCraw, Thomas K. 2007. *Prophet of Innovation: Joseph Schumpeter and Creative Destruction*. Cambridge, MA: Belknap.

McLuhan, Marshall. 2005. *Understanding Me: Lectures and Interviews*. Cambridge, MA: MIT Press.

Myers, David G. 2002. *Intuition: Its Powers and Perils*. New Haven, CT: Yale University Press.

Norman, Donald. 2003. *Emotional Design: Why We Love (or Hate) Everyday Things*. New York: Basic Books.

Putnam, Robert D. 2000. *Bowling Alone: The Collapse and Revival of American Community*. New York: Simon & Schuster.

Reich, Robert B. 2007. *Supercapitalism: The Transformation of Business, Democracy, and Everyday Life*. New York: Knopf.

Schumpeter, Joseph A. (1942) 2006. *Capitalism, Socialism and Democracy*. New York: Routledge.

Sennett, Richard. 1992. *The Conscience of the Eye: The Design and Social Life of Cities*. New York: W. W. Norton.

Steiner, Frederick, and Robert Yaro, eds. 1998. *To Heal the Earth: Selected Writings of Ian L. McHarg*. Washington, DC: Island Press.

Surowiecki, James. 2004. *The Wisdom of Crowds*. New York: Doubleday.

Susanka, Sarah. 1998. *The Not So Big House*. Newtown, CT: Taunton.

Watters, Ethan. 2004. *Urban Tribes: Are Friends the New Family?* New York: Bloomsbury USA.

INDEX